Quarterly Essay

1	FIRING LINE Australia's Path to War *James Brown*

69	CORRESPONDENCE *Clare O'Neil, Andrew Charlton, Jim Chalmers, Tom Bentley, Jonathan West, Bob Katter, Saul Eslake, Paul Strangio, Elizabeth Humphrys, Tad Tietze, Henry Sherrell, Verity Firth, George Megalogenis*

105	Contributors

Quarterly Essay is published four times a year by Black Inc., an imprint of Schwartz Publishing Pty Ltd. Publisher: Morry Schwartz.

ISBN 978-1-86395-841-7 ISSN 1832-0953

ALL RIGHTS RESERVED.
No part of this publication may be reproduced, stored in a retrieval system, or transmitted in any form by any means electronic, mechanical, photocopying, recording or otherwise without the prior consent of the publishers.

Essay & correspondence © retained by the authors.

Subscriptions – 1 year print & digital
(4 issues): $79.95 within Australia incl. GST.
Outside Australia $119.95. 2 years print & digital
(8 issues): $129.95 within Australia incl. GST.
1 year digital only: $39.95.

Payment may be made by Mastercard or Visa, or by cheque made out to Schwartz Publishing. Payment includes postage and handling.

To subscribe, fill out and post the subscription card or form inside this issue, or subscribe online:

www.quarterlyessay.com
subscribe@blackincbooks.com
Phone: 61 3 9486 0288

Correspondence should be addressed to:

The Editor, Quarterly Essay
Level 1, 221 Drummond Street
Carlton VIC 3053 Australia
Phone: 61 3 9486 0288 / Fax: 61 3 9011 6106
Email: quarterlyessay@blackincbooks.com

Editor: Chris Feik. Management: Caitlin Yates. Publicity: Anna Lensky. Design: Guy Mirabella. Assistant Editor: Kirstie Innes-Will. Production Coordinator: Siân Scott-Clash. Typesetting: Tristan Main.

FIRING LINE | *Australia's Path to War*

James Brown

Before I went to Hiroshima I did not know the word hypocentre. It didn't exist for me until I found it on a wall in the Hiroshima Peace Memorial Museum, past the diorama of children with charred skin flaps hanging from their outstretched arms. But there, hanging a precise distance above the clean model of a cityscape, was a polished plastic red ball: the hypocentre of the nuclear fireball of August 1945.

Before I went to North Korea and stood in a red-lit burial chamber to stare at the forever-set face of Kim Jong-il I had never felt the chill of a regime that could pull you aside, beat out your teeth and swallow you whole. Under the attentive gaze of his son's soldiers and henchmen, in that high-vaulted room displaying his body, I understood what it was to feel insignificant, impuissant – my existence the whim of someone else's machinations and politics.

Before I went to the Solomon Islands I had never peered down into the hull of a warship sunk with all hands and understood what it meant to be part of a great armada engaged in a desperate struggle. Nor seen what it meant for a finely crafted military campaign to be suddenly stopped, with either stratagem or luck snuffing out the lives of the defeated.

Before I went to Beirut I had not understood that in the space of two decades a beautiful city could decay, wracked by war and ruin, riven by rivalries. That law and order and commerce could give way to rule by gang. That life could mean rising every day to look south at a neighbouring valley with pure hatred.

Before I went to Iraq I had not tasted dust swept by desert winds from the top of a grave packed deep with hundreds of bodies – the remains of those who had refused to go on fighting Saddam's war against Iran. Nor sipped cool water inside the armour of a vehicle driving through a suburb thick with fighters wanting nothing more than to kill people like me.

Before I went to Afghanistan I had never listened to men calmly discuss the calibrated effect of their plans for the casual murder of civilians.

And before I came home to Australia from these places I had never really understood what it means to live in a place of bright skies and open minds. When you live in a country like ours, the dirty business of war is a stranger. That is the blessed legacy of a place where soldiers are rarely seen, and then only on parade. Where war means Anzac Day, and Anzac Days are all the same. There are few moments in modern Australia when you might pause to ask the most consequential of questions – a question that probes a nation's heart, scours its mind and resets the rhythm of its citizens' lives.

What is it that we are willing to fight for?

For what principles, what positions, would we stand up and never give in, no matter how great the struggle and how large the cost? And just as importantly, for what would we not fight? On what issues would we stand down, pack up our arms, decide to compromise or to walk away from a fight that is not ours? It is the most important question that governments and the people who elect them might ever have to answer. It is a question that is becoming more difficult for Australians to consider.

For much of Australia's history, the sliding and shifting tectonic plates of geopolitics have positioned our continent far from global strife. And in any case, we did not have the authority to decide on war, vested as it was in the hands of the colonial redcoat governors and successive British governments. The question of organising for national defence was at the heart of Henry Parkes' Tenterfield Oration and the planning for federation. But Australia herself only decided for war after the Statute of Westminster and the successive declarations of our governor-general in 1942 against Bulgaria and Thailand. Three years later the power to declare war, outside of an attack on our own borders, was largely surrendered to the United Nations. In the years since, some would argue, the decision has been ceded to our great ally the United States.

Perhaps for many Australians the answer is simple. We fight for all that lies within the white wash of waves breaking against our shore, the boundary of our sea-girt nation. That line on our mental map is clear and stark, the idea of physical invasion a natural concept for a country schooled to picture history as a series of landings of boats ashore: be it Botany Bay or Gallipoli. But that mental line has moved further and further outwards, pushed by myriad factors since 1945. The 1982 United Nations Convention on the Law of the Sea stretched the line far out beyond the crashing surf and into an exclusive economic zone extending 200 nautical miles in all directions. A deep blue inkblot of sovereignty leaches into the Indian Ocean, north to Timor, east by New Zealand and the Pacific Islands, south across the Antarctic. At 27.2 million square kilometres, Australia's jurisdictional claim on the earth's surface is the largest of any country in the world.

The ambitions of a prosperous country in a globalising world blur and broaden the lines of our security, too. A country like ours, dependent on trade across the oceans, necessarily has veins that extend inwards, outwards and across borders: free-flowing lines carrying energy, food, ideas, stories and relationships. An interconnected country linked by cables draped across the ocean floor: digital highways carrying the traffic to connect our financial transactions as well as our medical researchers. Modern Australia breathes because planes can ascend from Tullamarine, circle the planet and glide to a landing at Heathrow, John F. Kennedy or Shanghai.

Because oil can decant through the Strait of Hormuz into Singapore and Taiwan, then trickle down through the Indonesian archipelago to fill sedans and shops and shelves. Because satellites above can blink signals scheduling trains across the Nullarbor or surveying fires in the Pilliga. Our way of life, on reflection, is a surprisingly intricate thing. An exquisite thing, dependent on a fine global web of collaborations. A system of transactions anchored by trust and stability. Australia's security depends on lifelines that run from here across the planet.

For all the wonder of our connected, enlightened, prosperous age, the fundamental tenets of war remain largely the same as when laid down by Clausewitz, the German who is to war what Adam Smith is to economics. War is a political act, the deployment of violence to achieve an aim or avert a catastrophe. The character of warfare, though, is changing fast. The great strategists will tell you that warfare is evolving to take new and often unexpected forms: the horrors of ISIS are but one incarnation of the complexities and potency of newly globalised violence. But there is also a spectral reappearance of forms of violence long thought vanquished. The possibility of war between major powers, slight though it might be, is creeping back into the deliberations of Moscow, Beijing and Washington. The kind of war our grandparents faced has not yet been eradicated from our lives.

It would not be right to say that Australians cannot think about war when they need to. We have done so with passion, evidenced as much by the graves strewn through Western Europe as by the hundreds of thousands who marched in our streets both for East Timor and against Iraq. Some of our fiercest public debates have been on issues forced by war: conscription, nuclearised alliances, the dilemmas of choosing between forward defence and self-reliance. On whether we should meet the problems of the world head-on, or wait for them to make their way south. These debates are foundational to the way we think about war when provoked, but some of their core assumptions are now ageing badly. Tens of thousands of Australian soldiers have deployed to Iraq, Afghanistan, East Timor, the Solomon Islands and beyond in the past twenty years. The histories of these conflicts are just now beginning to be written. These conflicts have rightly shaped the way the public and parliament think about war – that is, when they think about it at all. But have they shaped our deliberations on war in the right ways?

It is a trope of history to criticise the generals who prepared to fight the last war and were caught out by new battlefields they could not comprehend. The French officers of World War I, resplendent in their scarlet pantaloons on battlefields sown grey with munitions and mud. The Maginot Line and its ineffectiveness against the armoured Blitzkrieg columns of Nazi Germany. But publics, too, can assume the next war will be like the last one.

In Australia's bright and blessed circumstances today, we rarely think of war: it is something we go to, not something that comes to us. It seems we often shrink from talking about war in any detailed way, as if to speak of evil might set us on an inevitable path towards it. And in the few moments when we publicly discuss or politically deliberate on new wars, our involvement in Iraq seems to set the template for our imagining of what war should or should not be. That's problematic, because warfare is rapidly evolving and remains a possibility – particularly within our region. Many of the intellectual frameworks and assumptions we retain from Iraq no longer hold, particularly those regarding the United States. As the Australian Defence Force spends billions of dollars on new equipment and facilities, building a grander military to insure against an uncertain future, the public remains largely mired in the past, blind to the new realities of strategic rivalry between our friends and allies. Our mechanisms for going to war lack the institutional rigour necessary to navigate a more complex world, and our decisions about conflict are not grounded by public trust and democratic legitimacy. We need urgently to re-engage with the problems of war, and to rethink just how it is that we choose whether we fight or not.

There is, perhaps rightly, little in the cabinets of the Hiroshima Peace Memorial Museum to explain how Hiroshima came to have a hypocentre.

It is only as you leave the building that you find a trace of historical context. "The conflict began," reads a small plaque beneath interviews with atomic survivors, "when the tensions between Japan and China of 1931 boiled over in 1937." It is a salient reminder that the seeds of war are usually sown long before any crisis, and that the signs of war may be apparent years in advance. Thinking seriously about war, intelligently preparing for the possibility, does not inevitably set us on a path towards it. But it does mean we do not approach problems unprepared.

My regimental commanding officer in Southern Iraq gave me a piece of advice before my troop headed out on our first mission: move like doves, think like hawks. It has stuck with me for the last decade; it should stick with you for the next one.

CROSSING THE LINE

In the early days of 2005 the conflict in Iraq is at a tipping point. January brings an election for the National Assembly of Iraq and a sense that a stable government might be formed. Three thousand expat Iraqis around Australia join their compatriots in casting votes. But the thickening insurgency in and around Baghdad portends that stability is slipping. On 26 January more American soldiers are killed in Iraq than on any day in the preceding two years. The Australian foreign-policy realist Owen Harries deplores American adventurism and declares that the experiment in Iraqi democracy will fail. Prime Minister John Howard argues that Australia, as a good international citizen, has a responsibility to help push the situation the right way, to help ensure that the Coalition now responsible for Iraq's transition holds firm. Among many emerging problems in the Coalition, there is one of particular interest to Australia. In southern Iraq's Al Muthanna province a Japanese reconstruction group is building hospitals, schools and water facilities, but because of the Japanese constitutional commitment to non-aggression, it relies on a nearby Dutch battalion for protection. The Dutch government has decided not to renew the deployment of its troops, and their departure threatens the continued Japanese presence. Should Japan withdraw, the credibility of the international Coalition in Iraq could be weakened at a critical time; damage will be done at both a strategic and tactical level.

In Washington, Australian officials learn of the problem posed by the Dutch withdrawal. The Japanese angle is important for a number of reasons. Conscious of China's growing power in East Asia, Australia is seeking Japan's support to join a nascent diplomatic grouping known as the East Asia Summit. The Al Muthanna deployment is an opportunity to help both Japan and the United States. To boot, it is in a quiet rural province: the risk to Australian soldiers will be relatively small. And they will be under the overall command of a British divisional headquarters, which Australians have historically preferred to US command. Australia in one move can help its allies Britain and America and provide immediate and tangible support as well as political relief to its embryonic partner Japan.

The diplomatic groundwork laid, formal correspondence commences between Prime Minister Howard, the Japanese prime minister, Junichiro Koizumi, and the British prime minister, Tony Blair. A request is made of Australia to deploy additional forces to Iraq, and this is deliberated on by the National Security Committee of Cabinet on 16 February 2005. Six days later Howard announces to assembled reporters the formation of the Al Muthanna Task Group, a 450-strong unit drawn from the army's 1st Brigade at Robertson Barracks, in whose auditorium my soldiers and I learn from the TV that we will go to war in ten weeks. We will have two missions, the first to "provide a secure environment for the Japanese engineering and support services which are ... involved in matters related to road and school construction, water availability, and also incidental health services," the second to train Iraqi security forces and help them to shepherd Iraq into a stable and secure future. Howard acknowledges the benefits of working closely with an Asian partner in Iraq, and the consequences for the international Coalition should Japan cease its reconstruction efforts and withdraw from the country. He acknowledges the "heavy burden" being shouldered by US and UK forces and concludes, "This decision and this deployment are consistent with Australia's strategic interests and with the best traditions of our forces."

The decision is ushered through parliament two weeks later. Eighteen questions are asked during Question Time. Five are on interest rates, but one is a Dorothy Dixer which allows the foreign minister, Alexander Downer, to confirm that the deployment will be under the auspices of UN Security Council Resolution 1546 and to argue, "Australia is not just a small, regional player; Australia is a significant country with a significant contribution to make to the world, not just its region." Howard repeats for the parliament what he told the press the day before. Opposition leader Kim Beazley slams the announcement as a breach of Howard's election promise, made only four months earlier, not to increase Australia's commitment. Howard acknowledges this, stating that circumstances have changed. In response, Beazley invokes Ben Chifley's critical response to the deployment of troops during World War II: "The Labor Opposition would not be doing its duty if it allowed the government to stride blunderingly into error in seven-league boots and then to seek to hide behind a smokescreen of patriotism or to seek to deflect criticism from themselves by talking of the gallantry of our soldiers." Beazley points to the lack of an exit strategy and the potential for deeper Australian involvement, and concludes that Australia should not commit forces permanently outside Southeast Asia, Australia's area of immediate strategic interest. Debate is brief, and the leader of the house, Tony Abbott, moves that the House of Representatives acknowledge the prime minister's statement. That done, the parliament returns to debating a petition on mobile-phone coverage received from the 354 residents of Marble Bar, Western Australia.

My path has been set to war.

*

Pick up spare glasses.
    Sell my car.
    Sew name tags onto my desert cams.
    iPod.
    Get road signs made for vehicles.
    Buy Monopoly for the guys going by boat.
    Power of attorney and will.
    The vehicles are ASLAVs – Australian Light Armoured Vehicles, but most people would call them tanks. Camouflaged boxes of armour on wheels, each with a whizzing turret and cannon. The technical data sticks in my head a decade later, just as the trainers intended. Fourteen tonnes combat-laden, amphibious, top speed 120 km/h, with two 7.62-mm machine guns, two banks of grenade launchers, three radios, and powered by a big Detroit Diesel 56VT engine. A laser to determine the range to a target, feed it into an on-board computer and spit out a firing solution

for the 25-mm Bushmaster chain gun that the gunner seated beside me controls with a small black joystick. Stuffed below our feet dangling in the turret cage are ammunition, water, explosives, food, medicine, oil, fuel, fire extinguishers, and all manner of miscellaneous items tucked into crevices and stowed with near-nautical precision. And on everything, sand. In our weapons, in our ears and in our faces as we drive north to war.

There are twenty-seven vehicles like this in our convoy, carried from Darwin on a ship named the HMAS *Tobruk*, commissioned for the Australian military five years before I was born. After we pick them up from the port of Kuwait, a stinking sea of oil pipelines and scalding metal, acrid fumes and relentless heat, we drive them down the smooth highways of Kuwait City to a humming tent city located just far enough into the desert to escape attention. Through yet more checkpoints we come to streets of air-conditioned hundred-man tents, small plazas of fast-food shops, gyms, dining facilities and serviced latrines. A living city with South Koreans, Japanese, Romanians, Californians – and now Australians. A "life support area" in the parlance of the American military bureaucracy. A place to wait, plan and prepare for the journey into Iraq.

On the night before we begin, I sit in a tent poring over the maps that will guide us into our area of operations. There are eleven in all, to cover an advance of 435 kilometres to the major US airbase at Tallil, inside Iraq. I have two small devices that I picked up at a Dick Smith Electronics store before leaving Darwin. One is a pocket dictaphone for recording detail during our patrols. I figure it is better to keep my head up and eyes out than to duck down to write in my notebook. The second is a pen-like digital measuring wheel that I use to trace our route through the maps. Each click marks another kilometre into Mesopotamia. I've been clicking back and forth obsessively for hours over strange place names – Basra, Batha, Al Khidr, Navistar, Safwan – measuring each unknown stretch of the road to be navigated.

Our intelligence briefing reports that a group of extremists have been detained at the Kuwait–Iraq border; further north there have been vehicle hijackings and bombings. The insurgents have found a cache of US military uniforms, making their suicide bombers harder to detect as they approach Coalition patrols. Their car-bombers have been putting female mannequins in passenger seats to make them less obvious. Improvised explosive devices (IEDs) are being found in sheep carcasses dumped on the sides of roads or hidden in culverts. Highway bridges are a prime threat, our intelligence corporal tells us, and insurgents like to drop bombs and grenades into the hatches of armoured vehicles as they pass underneath. Speed up and change lanes under the bridge to confuse them, and make sure one of your vehicles has its cannon at six o'clock, ready to fire, he suggests.

My gunner and driver are prepping and loading the ASLAV. I am clicking that little wheel from bridge to bridge on Iraq's superb but now deadly highway system. Memorise every aspect of the road, I reason: distances to highway exits, parallel routes in case the road is blocked or an ambush is reported. Measure how far between Coalition boundaries so we know which military units to call for help, so we can avoid poor coordination that might lead to fratricide. How far between fuel points? How far between towns? I'm craving precision, mapping the unknown, wanting to maximise our chances of getting out of trouble. Click, click, click.

We have our mission, always read twice, always in capital letters: "THE AMTG IS TO DEPLOY FM CAMP VIRGINIA TO FOB'S (SMITTY AND TALLIL) IOT COMMENCE SECURITY SECTOR REFORM BY 03 MAY 05 IN SPT OF THE JIRSG AND ISF." AMTG is us: the Al Muthanna Task Group. Camp Virginia is the American tent city, FOB's Smitty and Tallil are the forward operating bases to which we will be deploying. One is located on a vast American airbase by the ancient tombs of Ur, the other is just outside the southern Iraqi town of As Samawah and will be my home for the next six months. JIRSG is the Japanese Iraq Reconstruction and Support Group. ISF is the Iraqi Security Forces. Every mission has a reason, an "in order to." Ours is to commence security-sector reform. Put more plainly: train up the Iraqi army and stop bad things from happening in our area of operations.

We have discussed and planned for every contingency we can imagine. Refuelling, breakdown, getting separated, getting lost, getting attacked, casualties (our own and civilian). We have plans for when to rest, and even for how to drink enough water to defeat the 50-degree heat. We know the precise chain of command if our leaders are killed or disabled. We have a route: ASR Dallas to Ironhorse Rd, MSR Tampa to Navistar, ASR circle to the Safwan bypass, Black bridge bypass to Cedar II/Tallil, turn onto ASR Jackson, through Al Batha, Al Khidr to As Samawah. Turn left at the railyards. To simplify we decide on control words to report on the radio as we pass major points: "EAGLES DARE," "RESTING WOMBAT," "BOXING KANGAROO," "FAT TIGER." My squadron group is named Combat Team Eagle after our mascot, a lackadaisical eagle probably asleep in a cage back at Robertson Barracks. The tiger is the mascot of the infantry we are carrying.

Now we are ready. Shaved, showered, dressed and packed. In my front pockets are tourniquets and special bandages made of some sort of shellfish, which will quickly seal blast and bullet wounds. My official passport is tucked into my body armour, so too dog tags with my blood type. My trouser pockets are stuffed with cheat sheets for weapons systems, radios, codes, frequencies and call signs for the UK's 20th Armoured Infantry Brigade in Basra, which will dispatch medical evacuation helicopters to us if we need them. There are templates for issuing complex orders for elaborate missions, calling in artillery and close air support. Notebooks with the contact details for my men's families, girlfriends, wives (one of the men has both). Pistol, rifle, helmet, blast goggles, shemagh. I pull on my fire-resistant gloves.

A roar of engines and a snake of vehicles passes through security checkpoints and onto Route 80. We wind around fuel trucks and open lorries taking Bangladeshi contractors to construction sites. Closer to the Iraq border the traffic thins until it is only us. On the left a giant tank-proof ditch runs the whole way to Saudi Arabia. Ahead in no man's land is a sort of official roadhouse with hundreds of fuel tankers waiting to be cleared through. Following a yellow line, we cross a small bridge, drive past a partially manned checkpoint, and we are in the land between two of the most storied rivers of antiquity, the Euphrates and the Tigris. We are officially in a war zone. In these mud huts dotted with satellite TV dishes are people who want to kill us. With 326 kilometres to our base I key the radio switch and call "FAT TIGER."

Click.

THE IRAQ TEMPLATE

Much as I try, it is hard to place my personal experience of the Iraq War within the national political discourse. It is thirteen years now since that international wound was opened. At best it was a tragic mistake, taking thousands of military and civilian lives and disrupting entire nations. At worst, a deliberate and evil calculation, fuelling and fostering conflicts still claiming hundreds of thousands of lives right now. "The greatest disaster in American foreign policy," in the judgment of Madeleine Albright.

The youngest recruits joining the ADF today would have been but four years old when Australian soldiers, sailors and aircrew joined the campaign to invade Iraq in 2003. It's gone on long enough for me to have deployed there twice, as well as to a handful of other places. For Australia to have had had six governments, five prime ministers and eight defence ministers. I can see where Iraq hangs in our national consciousness, a spectre looming over every discussion of war and how Australia makes its way in the world.

Three perspectives colour my experience of the Iraq War. First, what was political for my contemporaries was all too tactical for me. While others were analysing the ebb and flow of arguments for and against the war, I was busily preparing to take part in it. I spent the first eighteen months of the war in training, watching fellow officers and soldiers board planes bound for Baghdad and wondering when my turn would come. What little I experienced then of the politics of the Iraq War was also unusually personal. John Howard is not an abstract political figure to me; he is the father of one of my closest friends. And in a small way that may have made the war more personal for him too: a briefing on a new and lethal IED technique, of the kind Howard received when he visited southern Iraq, must be more compelling when you can picture a person it is being used against. Since then, working on defence issues – in and out of the ADF – I have come to know many others in Canberra and Washington who took crucial decisions or made recommendations which shaped the 2nd Cavalry Regiment's way to war in 2005. I have also spoken to activists who made their own way to Baghdad in the early days of the bombing to act as human shields, to offer their bodies as well as their words. I can't understand their decision or agree with their perspective, but I respect their passion and their principles.

Alongside the tactical and the personal, there is the emotional. A decision to join the military is to invest your life in a duty you think important. More than a year of my life was absorbed by Australia's mission in Iraq, so my natural inclination is to conclude that it had some worth and was a meaningful endeavour. All of this is to say that in trying to understand how Australia decided to go to war in 2003 and how that decision has shaped every Australian military deployment since then, I bring biases which have both sharpened my focus and filtered my gaze.

I have only a few remnants of my first deployment to Iraq: some sandy camouflage uniforms, notebooks and maps in a green trunk rarely opened. My Iraq photos have faces in them, Iraqi and Australian, which are becoming harder to match with names and stories. Earlier this year, when a series of car bombs ripped through the southern Iraqi city of As Samawah, on whose outskirts I lived for six months, I wondered what had become of the locals who helped us navigate its streets and markets. There was the wise-cracking interpreter Ali, with his American college education and baseball cap to match, who was forced to stay in Iraq and find a job because his father refused to return his passport. The endearing Muhammad, working to keep his seven children in school and safe. Only a few were relocated to Australia as refugees. There is a Facebook page for the Al Muthanna Task Group, which is planning a reunion later this year. Among its members, those soldiers still serving show the wear and tear of commuting to the Middle East for the better part of ten years. Subtle signs point to two who have killed themselves in the past twelve months. Suicide among veterans is a scourge that seems mostly to claim the young, although no one in Australia yet has the data to know for sure. Already in the first half of this year several young veterans have hanged themselves behind barrack-room doors in Townsville and Darwin.

Against the global costs of the great tragedy of Iraq, and the personal cost to those soldiers I deployed with and their families, there rests the question of whether our deployment was worthwhile, whether it advanced Australia's interests. To be sure, my troops and I had small successes. We kept the Japanese engineer battalion secure and their work building hospitals and schools went ahead largely unimpeded. We sometimes salved tensions in Al Muthanna province, and through our patrolling and training temporarily strengthened security so that battered locals could live slightly more normal lives. On occasions, where we could, we directly helped Iraqis. But there were also occasions when we made the assessment that we could not help.

My rotation of troops came away from southern Iraq with no casualties. Some would argue that this was the result of precise calculation, Australian leaders making a canny tactical contribution to a quiet corner of the Coalition campaign in order to minimise the risk to Australian soldiers. There is an element of truth to that: we could have been deployed to a province such as Anbar, or to what eventually became a ghoulish British purgatory in Basra. But luck plays such a large part in war that I am reluctant to ascribe too much strategic acuity to the avoidance of losses among our number. It seems likely that our deployment contributed to the strengthening of Australia's relationships with Japan, the United Kingdom and the United States. It's bleak but necessary to acknowledge that we certainly became better soldiers because of our involvement, better able to understand our profession, the wiles of adversaries and the ways of allies.

But the success or otherwise of Australia's military strategy in Iraq has barely been parsed, the effectiveness of our military contribution barely assessed at the operational level. Instead, the Iraq debate in Australia hangs on two sharp political questions: whose fault was it that we joined the campaign, and how did it come about? What little formal reflection on

Iraq there has been in Australia has focused on these areas. The Flood Inquiry examined the capacity and independence of Australia's intelligence agencies, and the Campaign for an Iraq War Inquiry has argued for a comprehensive investigation of the steps that led to Australia's decision to go. The reforms advocated have been correspondingly specific. The Flood Inquiry recommended additional resources for the prime minister's intelligence agency, and the Campaign for an Iraq War Inquiry supports legislation requiring parliamentary approval for deployment to war. Both of these examinations of Iraq, though important, are lopsided. Analysing the intelligence that led to Iraq neglects consideration of the military strategy that followed the political decision to join the campaign. Advocating for greater parliamentary approval for the deployment of troops does not address the ongoing role for parliament in scrutinising and evaluating the conduct of a war.

Australia's examination of both the decision to go to Iraq and the conduct there of its defence force has been much narrower than that in the United States and United Kingdom. In the US, the Iraq Study Group and legions of congressional, executive, academic and think-tank reports have assessed the conflict at every level: from the oft-bloated development contracts to the lightning special forces raids. So too has the UK comprehensively reviewed the war, from the perspective of the parliament, the public and the executive (although it still awaits the delivery of the Chilcot Inquiry). But in Australia, the ADF has spent comparatively little time learning lessons from the deployment of thousands of troops over five years. An official war history has just been commissioned; if past form is any guide, it will be at least a decade before it is completed, and in any event its brief is to recount what took place, not to reflect on whether it was the best course of action for Australia.

There are legitimate questions to be asked about Australia's military strategy in Iraq: how it was that the mission slowly crept forward and Australia chose to commit more troops over time, whether our military officers became so close to their US counterparts that they could not distinguish between Coalition interests and our own, what benchmarks for success were set by the government and whether they were achieved, and what the true cost to Australia of sending troops was. But they have not been asked, nor satisfactorily answered. Few concrete solutions have been proposed. Instead, they await the conclusion of an interminable grand political debate, with its highly charged, often ideological positions. As a result, our thinking on how we go to war has barely evolved: Iraq remains the template for how Australia responds to any new crisis that might require military deployment. Nowhere has this been more obvious than in Canberra's deliberations on going to war against ISIS in Iraq and Syria.

The decision on deploying to Iraq in 2014 couldn't have been more different from that facing Australia in 2003. For a start, there was an urbane liberal professor of constitutional law in the White House rather than a blunt neoconservative. America was weary of war and reluctant to engage further in the Middle East. The threat to Western nations from ISIS and its foreign fighters was clear and direct. The international Coalition assembled to fight included France and Canada, which had both declined to invade in 2003. And this time it was not an invasion, but rather a response to an invitation (albeit grudgingly issued) from Baghdad to send troops into its territory. Yet the discussion in the Australian parliament and media played out as if nothing had changed in the intervening decade. The government applied the template military response to requests from our ally to join an international coalition: the deployment of special forces. It applied the template political approach of being coy on military strategy, mission objectives and timelines, tying itself in knots to make abstract the potential cost of military action by promising "no boots on the ground." The Opposition focused solely on the status of the conflict under international law, either unwilling or unable to follow through with questions connecting military options to political objectives. The Greens labelled it "another war in Iraq," and the media applied their Iraq template too, asking about mission creep and hidden agendas.

From the obvious failures of Iraq, and having little familiarity with the military, many Australians have drawn conclusions that shape their thinking about any future conflict. They see wars abroad as discretionary and judge that Australia does not need to make a contribution. They do not expect governments to articulate clear military objectives and in fact are prepared for the conduct of military campaigns to be quite opaque. Appreciating that the United States is neither omniscient nor omnipotent, they are concerned that supporting its strategies might lead to more harm than good. And so, for each situation in which Australia is called upon to use military force, they apply a template that has not shifted since 2003.

The legacies of Iraq flow through to our deliberations on international policy and Australia's place in the world, as they should. But they are instincts, not insights. And when it comes to the geopolitics playing out in Asia right now, they are blinding.

BLIND INTO BEIJING

You can't see Asia from Darwin, but you can sense it, splashed through the jackfruit and market laksas, seeping from the eaves of open houses and leeching down the city's air-conditioned towers soaked by mid-afternoon downpours. Asia's history saturates Darwin too. Catalogued in the fine museum that sits on Fannie Bay are small boats in which tribes, some long gone, plied the inlets and waterways of Southeast Asia. Dotted everywhere are reminders of Australia's conflicts past: a Timorese gift shop near Nightcliff beach, the hulk of the US Navy's destroyer *Peary* on Darwin Harbour's sandy bottom, the enormous sleeping B-52 bomber beside Darwin airport, Australia's most northerly military airfield. Asia's future laces the town too. In Darwin Harbour the hulking tanks and terminals of the $47-billion Ichthys project are working to ship gas north to light homes in Tokyo, Osaka and Kansai. Perched on a cliff above it is the large Indonesian consulate, whose consul feverishly tweets his daily efforts to bring Australia and Indonesia closer together. Geography is playing its part too; every year Darwin is moving centimetres closer to Asia.

It's a different town from the one I lived in a decade ago as an intemperate junior army officer posted to the cavalry regiment there. Many of my former colleagues have never left Darwin, seduced by its sultry quirkiness and simple civics. Military activities there are more real-time than those further south: soldiers are on standby for contingencies, and ships conduct operational patrolling. And in Darwin the shifting power relativities of Asia are playing out. The city is not a strategic crossroads in the sense of World War II Lisbon, Cold War Vienna or, for that matter, the Dubai of the War on Terror. The height of Darwin intrigue remains the unknown motivations of a recent lord mayor who embezzled taxpayer funds to secure a $910 fridge, women's underwear, a punching bag and a *Star Wars*–themed voice modulator. But all the same, it is in Darwin that you can run your hand along the seams of Australia's American alliance.

President Obama's 2011 visit to the city was like nothing its residents had ever seen. Standing on a flag-bedazzled stage at the Royal Australian Air Force base alongside Prime Minister Julia Gillard, he laid the first policy block of the new US pivot to Asia: a taskforce of 2500 US marines was to be based in Darwin, replete with tanks, helicopters, artillery and amphibious tractors. The soldier friends I spotted in the assembled crowd were clapping, but didn't seem certain exactly what it was they were celebrating.

The Australian and American presentation of the pivot to Asia had, in retrospect, some peculiar contradictions. Obama's preceding speech in Canberra framed US–China relations in strident terms, characterising political repression in China as a form of poverty and affirming that the US was "all in" when it came to Asia. The rock-concert staging of the announcement in Darwin flagged a desire to ensure it reverberated in Delhi, Hanoi, Tokyo, Jakarta and Beijing. But once the new measures were revealed, the Australian government seemed keen to usher the whole thing back behind the curtains, arguing alternately that the marine rotation was so minor as to be of no consequence, that it was designed merely to support Australian Army amphibious training, or that it was a form of economic stimulus for the Northern Territory. Instead, the narrative moved to the Asian Century White Paper, which barely engaged with Asia's geopolitics but saw trade opportunities stretching to the horizon.

The Australian government was not caught flat-footed by the Darwin announcement: indeed, it had been seeking renewed US engagement in Asia for most of the preceding decade. The presence of US troops in Australia had been mooted as early as 2003, part of a strategic American realignment in the Pacific. Australian governments had built joint training facilities in northern Australia with the US military in mind, and had sought to craft a more effective Asian diplomatic order by urging the United States to join the East Asia Summit. Australia had also supported Secretary of State Hillary Clinton in 2010, when she declared the peaceful resolution of South China Sea territorial disputes to be a US national interest. Indeed, it was Kevin Rudd who raised with President Obama the idea of military basing in Australia. Hence the degree of blowback in Australia to the Darwin announcement must have come as a surprise to Washington.

The US pivot to Asia, and especially Australia's role in it, was fitted to the Iraq template. Chinese activities in the South China Sea were largely out of sight to Australians. What was in view was the wind-down of the American-led wars in the Middle East, which had delivered little success but an increasing number of Australian casualties. In a lecture the year after the Darwin announcement, former prime minister Malcolm Fraser declared:

> If this scenario goes ahead, there would then be a fully rounded marine fighting unit based in Darwin over which we would have no control. Some Australians may think it is there for our defence. That would be another piece of mythology. What conceivable threat can we see to the mainland of Australia in today's world? That unit is there to serve the American policy of containment.

To him the US pivot to Asia was neoconservatism for a new age in a new military theatre of operations. In the same year Hugh White's excellent *The China Choice* provocation distilled the dilemma Australia would face in managing its traditional ally, the United States, alongside its new trade partner, China. But it also carried the message that in any long-term competition between China and the United States, the US would lose. Former prime minister Paul Keating was incensed by the Obama speech in Canberra, deeming it "an oral and policy assault on China and its polity." He concluded that the marine deployment to Darwin was propelled by little more than "regard for withering associations," and suggested that Australian support for the US pivot was contrary to our national interest in Southeast Asia. Two of Australia's most prominent billionaires, each doing extensive business in China, joined the chorus. "China has been a better friend to us than we've been to China," said James Packer. Kerry Stokes, the owner of one of Australia's three commercial TV networks and a valued donor to the Australian War Memorial, declared himself "physically repulsed by the thought of armed people on [our] soil not being under our command," and suggested Australia should aspire to be the "Switzerland of the region." Others warned of the potential economic cost of any disruption of the China relationship. The combination of two former prime ministers, a respected strategic thinker and senior business figures critiquing the deal was compelling. Australians became convinced that the United States was entangling us in a march to war with China, and surveys showed deep concern about joining US military action in Asia.

Australia's politicians, seldom comfortable discussing military strategic issues, did little to address the growing chorus of alarm. In fact, they did little to explain the measures agreed to with the United States at all. When Prime Minister Tony Abbott signed the Force Posture Agreement formalising the Darwin presence in June 2014, there was no accompanying attempt to explain to the public what it meant. In 2015, when a US official indicated in testimony before Congress that B-1 bombers might be bound for Australia, the Australian media went ballistic. Australian government officials scrambled to shut down the conversation, issuing denials that any such planning was taking place. A year later it became clear that even though there was no formal agreement, the presence of B-1 bombers in Australia was in fact up for discussion.

In 2012, as Fraser and Keating were setting the frame for public discussion of America's pivot to Asia, the US military was discussing a new military concept: "Air-Sea Battle." It called, among other things, for the dispersal of American aircraft from bases in Guam, Korea and Japan to elude China's growing long-range missile forces. It also outlined in detail how Chinese and American aircraft might encounter each other in the skies of East Asia, and discussed how Chinese long-range missile systems could be defeated by attacks on their command-and-control infrastructure. To Australian critics of the Darwin announcement, Air-Sea Battle was proof positive of a hidden strategy that aimed to do more than contain growing Chinese power: the United States planned to go to war against Beijing if necessary. Adding to the suspicion, in 2012 an Australian general was appointed to a position within America's Pacific Command at Honolulu responsible for considering conflict and crisis contingencies. The appointment only came to light when news of it was published in an American military service newspaper.

It is the burden of a superpower to think through conflict in detail, to consider how peace and prosperity might come to an end. Thinking about the possibility of war is also a particularly American preoccupation. Hundreds of reports are produced each year for the American military, concepts tested and plans shelved. Many of these are unclassified, produced by universities and think-tanks to provoke debate and stimulate policy development. Public debate on military issues, including interventions by senior officers, is remarkably franker in the United States than in Australia. If you want to find a carefully detailed exposition of a plan to blockade all naval traffic passing through the straits of Malacca or Hormuz, you can. Nothing about this is new – in the 1920s and 1930s, for example, the American military had a detailed plan, "War Plan Red," designed to isolate Australia and other Commonwealth countries in the unlikely event that Britain ever went to war with the United States again. Air-Sea Battle was crafted at the operational level, devoid of politics, and with a tin ear to regional sensitivities. A draftsman's concept that an architect might never chose to use. For all the discussion it generated, it was as likely to commit the United States to war against China (or Iran, for that matter) as War Plan Red had been to commit America to fight Australia before World War II. But in Australia, where defence concepts are rarely publicly discussed or debated, Air-Sea Battle fell with a clunk.

The elements of the Iraq template so concerning to many Australians had started to materialise. There was a government coy to discuss the strategic environment, its alliance activities and its objectives. There was preparation for a possible crisis or conflict in which Australia had no apparent stake, in which our involvement was largely discretionary, and which was somewhat prejudicial to our national interest. There was the view that bringing any sort of pressure to bear on China would ultimately be a failure and damage Australian interests. On top of this, there was a hidden plan for military conflict with Beijing.

This caricature remains prevalent. The business editor of a major Australian newspaper recently accused the Australian parliament of having "practically wet itself on a bipartisan basis in welcoming a regular US marine presence in Darwin," and concluded:

> "Pivot" is well short of George Bush's disastrous "Axis of Evil" name calling, but how did that pan out? It presaged escalating tensions and the Iraq war with all its unintended consequences. The pivot declaration and the escalated diplomatic and military policies that followed still amounted to a shot across China's bows. It's no wonder China responded.

But Australians need to look again. Five years after the Darwin announcement the dynamics in our region have become more transparent. How China intends to use its growing military and economic heft is becoming clearer.

ALTERNATE REALITIES

Although the probability of war in Asia is small, it is real. It is exercising minds in the Philippines, Vietnam and Japan, where recent surveys show that majorities consider war with a rising China a likely prospect in their lifetimes. Australians are more sanguine, but a third are convinced that China will pose a military threat to Australia in their lifetimes. China's military is now a capable and modern force. It is modernising and expanding its strategic missile forces, building more sophisticated nuclear weapons as well as more powerful missiles that can push them further. China is learning how to conduct aircraft-carrier operations, expanding its submarine fleet and operating naval taskforces further from home. China has modernised its command-and-control systems, developing new military jurisdictions and headquarters better suited to the possibility of war with its neighbours; its cyber-security services remain hyperactive and persistent, it operates a vast drone fleet, and it is developing weapons to be used in space to bring down American satellites. Of course, not all Chinese military activity is inherently concerning – a rising power should be expected to want to broaden and deepen what its military can do. China is now a leading contributor of peacekeepers to United Nations missions, operates ships combating piracy in the Indian Ocean, and is engaged in humanitarian assistance and disaster relief. It also increasingly participates in multinational military exercises and has conducted several with Australia, as well as with the United States.

In gauging the threat another country might present, defence planners assess two things: capability and intent. Capability can be observed and measured, and at almost every level China's military capability is increasing rapidly. Capability is more than just new weapons; it is also about the systems, training and procedures that allow you to use them. It took eighteen years, but China is now able to operate planes from its aircraft-carrier decks. But it is still a long way from being able to fight a war with carrier-based fighter aircraft, or use them to project credible power. Developing that capability has taken the United States ninety years, billions of dollars and the lives of more than fifty pilots lost to training accidents. But Chinese military capability is sufficiently advanced for it to dominate the approaches to its coastline out to the first island chain – Japan, Taiwan and the Philippines.

Intent is more malleable and less predictable. It relies on political deliberations that can change overnight, as well as over decades. In the past decade, Chinese thinking on how to use its growing military has shown alarming trends. Most of these can be seen in the emblematic issue of the South China Sea and the disputed islands and maritime features within it.

Since before the US pivot to Asia began, Chinese military and civilian vessels have been harassing and intimidating ships in areas of ocean contested with neighbours such as Vietnam, the Philippines and Indonesia. The tensions over the South China Sea islands and reefs are complex, legally bewildering, and confounded by shifting and overlapping histories dating back centuries. For decades China has manned small outposts on some of the islands; it infamously fought a short, sharp war with Vietnam over some of them in 1988. Now China is showing that it intends to consolidate control of disputed islands spread more than 1000 kilometres south of the Chinese mainland. Two new tactics have been particularly effective – the first is the use of civilian fishing vessels and white-hulled coastguard ships to bully ships from other countries. In one notorious incident in 2014, in which a Chinese oil drilling rig was moved into waters contested with Vietnam, it was protected by a circling flotilla of nearly eighty Chinese fishing boats as well as coastguard and naval vessels, which buffeted Vietnamese ships aside as they attempted to enforce their sovereignty.

China's second tactic has been to construct large fortresses on sea rocks and reefs throughout the South China Sea. It is an engineering feat as breathtaking as it is expensive. China is conjuring islands in the midst of shipping lanes. The speed of the effort is stunning. In just two years, more than 3200 acres of land have been terraformed to build runways capable of operating bombers, as well as radar systems to scan the air and detect the movement of any vessel or plane. The military equipment China is installing on some of these islands is highly advanced: a new missile system that can shoot at ships within a 400-kilometre radius; artillery pieces mounted on armoured vehicles capable of firing at approaching ships. The Chinese foreign minister has deflected criticism by Australia and others of this massive and provocative project by saying that the islands are there to provide public goods and are open to international citizens. But this remains far from convincing. As the secretary of Australia's Department of Defence, Dennis Richardson, put it in a lecture, "It is legitimate to ask the purpose of the land reclamation – tourism appears unlikely."

It can be hard for Australians to see why this construction in the South China Sea is concerning. But these island fortresses are akin to unexpected military checkpoints on one of the world's most important maritime highways. Sixty per cent of Australia's exports and 40 per cent of its imports travel through these waters. Introducing more troops and new weapons into areas already in dispute is inflammatory – the maritime equivalent of sending troops into Korea's demilitarised zone – and could cause tensions to flare. More broadly, as China increases its military power, it has less need to accommodate the needs of other countries in the region. Chinese leaders say they will never threaten freedom of navigation through the South China Sea, and logic says it is in China's interest not to interfere with international shipping. But China would nevertheless have the means to compete more aggressively for maritime resources and power within the South China Sea, should it choose.

The South China Sea issue should not be emblematic of the relationship between the United States and China, nor should maritime disputes between countries be this hard to settle. The US–China relationship is both rich and deep, with more than ninety official meetings each year and extensive people-to-people links, some extending back to the nineteenth century. In the past two years presidents Obama and Xi Jinping concluded a successful agreement on climate change, and one is likely soon on bilateral trade. And in our established system of international law and governance, many countries have resolved territorial disputes at sea, including Australia. Indeed, America once settled a dispute over islands contested with Britain by submitting the case to binding international arbitration. There are extensive provisions in international law that provide a path for ownership claims to be articulated and resolved, one of which is now being pursued by the Philippines with regard to its South China Sea claims. But China has refused to take any of these paths, and refused even to state the extent of its claims in the South China Sea. Instead, it has chosen to strengthen its hold through action, and that action has a distinctly nationalistic tone.

Overall, nationalism and militarism appear to be on the rise in China – particularly with regard to Japan, but also in the South China Sea. President Xi does not represent the entire aspirations of the Chinese people, but he clearly represents the current intent of the Chinese state. His leadership style is becoming more martial: he has dramatically consolidated his power over the People's Liberation Army, and last September presided over a grand parade in Beijing, heralding the arrival of the modern Chinese military. Wearing a dark boiler suit reminiscent of Mao, President Xi stood atop an open limousine beneath 200 thundering fighter jets, surveying 12,000 troops and assembled tanks and missile launchers. Earlier this year, he began wearing a military uniform with military-rank insignia to visit bases around China, a departure from the practice of recent Chinese leaders.

Even among the most sceptical analysts, there is little doubt now that the actions of Chinese maritime agencies in the South China Sea are being tightly coordinated and endorsed by China's leadership. These actions represent a more militarised, assertive strategy for the region, and confrontations between the United States and China now occur regularly. American warships heading into the South China Sea are hailed by Chinese naval warships, their intentions and their routes are questioned, and they are followed at a distance. The US Navy and other regional navies have responded by undertaking more freedom-of-navigation patrols, passages through the South China Sea designed to remind China of its obligations under the United Nations Convention on the Law of the Sea. These interactions are tightly choreographed and designed to make political points while demonstrating military restraint. Similarly, China is being careful to keep any provocations and probing in "the grey zone" – not aggressive enough to cross the threshold and be considered acts of war, but certainly above the normal threshold of peacetime interaction. Yet operating military platforms at close proximity can be dangerous. In May 2016, US and Chinese aircraft had an encounter at less than twenty metres – the type of encounter that led to loss of life and an international crisis in 2001, when Chinese pilots attempted to force an American surveillance plane from its course to nearby Chinese territory.

Perhaps China only intends to undermine and embarrass the United States temporarily in the region, perhaps it intends much more. In Singapore, Malaysia, New Zealand, Vietnam and Indonesia, leaders have come to the conclusion that China intends to use its newly powerful military muscle to jostle and sometimes bully its way to what it wants. That means defence planners must think through the future implications of Chinese aggression. That is happening in Japan, where the air force and navy are on heightened alert for intrusions into their territory by Chinese aircraft. It's happening in the Philippines, where the US military has been invited back to operate for the first time since it was asked to leave Subic Bay in 1992. It's happening in Vietnam, whose communist leader has tightened security and economic links with the United States.

Cheap access to commercial satellite technology means that China's development of island fortresses is increasingly visible at the click of a mouse, but it remains hard for Australians to see the long-term significance of the granular developments in the South China Sea. According to a survey published by the United States Studies Centre this year, just 4 per cent of Australians rated the South China Sea as the most important national security threat to Australia – they were troubled instead by the more visible threat of terrorism. But the potential for conflict in the South

China Sea should be of concern. Beyond their immediate effect, any hostilities would involve massive disruption to the finely calibrated trade networks in East Asia that underpin the prosperity we take for granted and that our Asian neighbours have come to appreciate. Beyond the damage to our trading partners, there would be a direct impact on Australia's economy were war to break out in the South China Sea: all our automotive gasoline comes from refineries in Taiwan, Korea and Singapore. All of this makes a major war in Asia one of the relatively low-probability but very high-impact risks that Australia cannot afford to ignore and needs to consider more seriously.

*

I'm in a heated conversation with a US deputy assistant secretary of state, who is pressing me to sign a declaration condemning China's recent actions in the South China Sea. The Philippines has already signed, its government alternating between fury and anxiety in response to near-constant harassment of their small military forces. India has deployed a number of ships to the region, operating from the Vietnamese port in Cam Ranh Bay. It seems China will be unable to be deterred from seizing more territory in the Spratly Islands. The United States is hopeful that if Australia signs the declaration, it may motivate others in the region, such as Indonesia, to join the chorus of condemnation and give China reasons to pause and reconsider. But I'm trying to unravel what the wider US strategy is: I've heard from the Japanese defence minister that along with the United States commencing preparations to move more aircraft carriers towards Japan, there are whispered suggestions that it might open discussions about positioning strategic missiles on the Japanese islands. That would be a calamitous move, an escalation of epic proportions, but it just might demonstrate to China how serious US resolve on this issue is. Or it could be that the Japanese defence minister has this wrong, or is trying to convince me that the US is more locked into escalating the issue than it truly is. What's clear is just how frequently the Japanese and Americans are talking. Most of

Australia's Beijing analysis is now being received second-hand – our defence liaison staff in the embassy there normally have counterparts that they can go to on the Oceania desk of the People's Liberation Army international department. But in this escalating crisis, these English speakers have been drafted to support their colleagues on the US desk. The sheer scale of activity, messaging and planning being generated by this crisis is overwhelming. Assessing options and developing plans to ward off further escalation is difficult when your immediate focus is trying to get enough time with allies and friends to understand the extent of the problem you are dealing with. I eventually find time to consult with Singapore, Malaysia and the Indonesian foreign minister before we break for dinner. As I leave the room, round the corner I find the North Korean and Chinese leaders screaming at each other over some sort of border incident.

It's a simulation, of course, but a useful one designed to plumb the darkest potentials of rivalry in Asia – even if these are somewhat difficult to contemplate in the warmth of the Southern California coast. The program is one of several funded by the New York–based philanthropist Roger Hertog, devised in the aftermath of disastrous decision-making on Iraq to foster a more rigorous approach to the problems of strategy. "What appeals to me about Grand Strategy," Hertog said in a 2008 interview, "is that these programs build a certain intellectual discipline rather than create an ideological partisanship."

The program culminates in a multi-day simulation: a sort of Risk meets Settlers of Catan exercise designed to allow the gaming out of various crises, strategies and decisions. It begins with an appreciation of how preposterous it is to casually discuss military deployments, tensions and conflict as if playing a board game. The pressure is artificial, decision-making time compressed, and some narrative developments seem absurd (all the more so when the academic role-playing Russia decides to adopt an accent for the duration of our discussion). But in time the dynamics give the tiniest sense of what chaos and conflict might look like. For a start, as Australia's representative I'm struggling to secure time with

American colleagues as they focus on their crisis negotiations with China. I'm relying more than I thought on Japan for counsel and information, and I'm much more focused on Southeast Asia than I'd expected. Russia, so far on the margins of my thinking about Asia, has real clout in the region with the military assets it can deploy and the arms deals it can provide. The regional alignment is shaking out rapidly too – countries are choosing to align themselves in a bipolar fashion with either the United States or China. Unsurprisingly, everyone wants to engage with Indonesia, which remains hard to read and somewhat aloof. When the game descends to war, as it does in about half the simulations, it eerily resembles the Pacific War of World War II.

We model many things in the universities of Australia – climate change, economics, finance, structural fatigue in buildings – but in very few courses do we model what war might look like. There are crisis simulations in a handful of international relations courses, but only at the Strategic and Defence Studies Centre of the Australian National University does more thoughtful simulation take place. For all our talk of the Asian century and the security dilemmas it might bring, we are barely equipping our best and brightest with the tools and perspectives they need to manage its tensions and risks.

If we are to consider deeply the possibility of war with China, then we must also probe our understanding of the Australian alliance with America. It is a distinctively close relationship – closer to a marriage than, say, America's alliance with Saudi Arabia, which is based on rawer calculations of mutual interest. The organisational and people-to-people connections that underpin the formal ANZUS security agreement are remarkably strong not just in the military, but also throughout society. Australian academics collaborate more with Americans than with any other nationality, so too artists and businesspeople. The scale of investment by American companies in Australia is colossal: they have invested more in developing Australia's gas fields, for example, than America invested in the Apollo 11 project.

Partly for this reason, Malcolm Fraser's call to end the alliance, as well as the local debate on China, have created ripples of anxiety among the custodians of ANZUS in recent years. Privately, US officials are curious to know on what issues Australia might diverge from the United States in the future – and on what issues we might say no. The ANU's Strategic and Defence Studies Centre recently described some of these anxieties at elite levels of the relationship:

> The Australian government tries to downplay suggestions that Australians must choose between China and the United States along the lines suggested by former Australian Prime Minister Malcolm Fraser. Yet in no other US-allied capital do former leaders engage in such blatant questioning of the alliance with the United States . . . These public debates by the United States' closest ally in the Pacific have some senior US officials quietly questioning whether Japan may in future replace Australia as the most trustworthy ally should US and regional tensions continue mounting with Beijing. In the midst of Asia's ascent today, however, it is Australians who worry about entrapment by Washington and Americans that worry about abandonment by Canberra.

It would not do to begin a marriage each day by clinically dissecting its strengths and weaknesses, or by canvassing alternative arrangements. But in any long-term relationship, it's prudent to reflect deeply every now and then on what might be, had different paths been chosen. In an alliance, based as it is on mutually recognised interests, a periodic stocktake is critical. Ironically, it took the rise of Donald Trump to make it more acceptable to consider the end of Australia's American alliance. In the past few months, views have come thick and fast presaging what a Trump presidency might mean for the alliance, and how a brash and erratic US foreign policy might stretch ANZUS past breaking point. But the rise of Trump has also reminded Australians that there are worse futures for Asia than one in which the United States is pivoting back to it.

Trump has twice now suggested he would be prepared to leave South Korea and Japan without the presence of the US military deployed in those countries. In an interview with the *New York Times*, Trump suggested it might be better for the United States if South Korea and Japan armed themselves with nuclear weapons to defend against China and North Korea. It was a salient reminder that the relative lack of nuclear proliferation in East Asia has not been an accident, but rather thanks to the patient and painstaking work of the world's largest military superpower – and its network of Asian alliances, which restrain and reassure the restless and fearful.

Ending the alliance would be enormously damaging for Australia. To begin with, it would be tremendously expensive. Malcolm Fraser's analysis concluded that if ANZUS were ended, Australia could match its levels of defence capability under the alliance by spending 3 per cent of GDP (up from 2 per cent at the moment). The reality is much starker. The late scholar Coral Bell provided a useful reference point with her findings that were European countries to withdraw from NATO, they might need to increase their defence spending four-fold. Given Australia's geography and expansive national interests, the assumption that we might need to spend an additional 4 to 6 per cent of GDP on defence to replace what the alliance currently provides does not seem outrageous. This would mean an enormous diversion of funding from health, welfare and education to give Australians the level of national security they have come to expect. More importantly, although it is important not to overstate Australia's access and influence in Washington, withdrawing from the alliance would give us no ability to shape the foreign policy of the world's largest power – whether to encourage American administrations to exercise more restraint, or to intervene in problems of consequence to us. Estranging ourselves from direct access to decision-makers within the administration of the world's most consequential power would be a bold choice indeed. Withdrawing from the alliance would also put us out of step with the fifty other countries around the world allied with the United States. Making a judgment to end the alliance would suggest our global interests and strategic judgments were in some crucial way different from those of the Cameron government in the United Kingdom, the Merkel government in Germany, and even the socialist party currently attempting to form government in Spain.

Public support for the alliance remains high in Australia, but its application in Asia yields more cautious results. As we have seen, Australians are worried about what it might mean to support the United States in a conflict within the region. Any Australian involvement in a conflict with China would most likely come about through a request from the United States, and it is difficult to imagine that the alliance would not suffer fundamental damage were Australia to refuse support in the event of such a confrontation.

So it has become critical to explore all the scenarios, including the less likely ones, in which Australia and America jointly decide to use military force somewhere in Asia. Beyond the region, Australia and America see security challenges in a very similar way. Within Asia, managing their distinct national interests is a more difficult and delicate task. Correspondingly, the tempo of strategic discussion between the defence officials of both countries has quickened. In 2012, for the first time in sixty years, Australia's military service leaders and the chief of the defence force spent time with their American counterparts to compare Pacific strategies. At the operational level Americans and Australians are also comparing and contrasting their regional defence diplomacy programs. And in table-top exercises, defence planners are mapping the limits of US and Australian interests – the expectation gaps and pressure points. The Australian perspective is not that of an over-eager junior partner. Instead, Australian officials are increasingly clear-eyed about what America wants, clearer on what is important to Australia, and more prepared to manage disagreement. A more sophisticated and pragmatic alliance is developing.

Increasingly, it seems Australia has most to offer the alliance acting within our region. America wants a primary responder to any issues arising in the Southwest Pacific and Papua New Guinea. It wants an ally with shared values and some standing that can help to shape norms and outcomes favourable to the US, particularly in Southeast Asia. Complementary to this is Australia's ability to provide useful perspectives, ideas and, sometimes, intelligence analysis. A sort of "sophisticated, friendly muse" on the region, as Kim Beazley describes it. America appreciates Australia's military and diplomatic contribution to problems in the wider world, but will be increasingly willing to trade this off for the certainty that, in case of need, Australia will provide a secure logistics hub and safe harbour, and a defence force that can reliably mount its own operations in the near-region.

Most of this evolution in the alliance is happening well beyond the public's gaze and has not found its way into the political discussion. The challenge is to bring more of us into this imagining of the scenarios and contingencies of Asia's future. Otherwise, the new arrangements which seek to balance Australia's independence and its alliance might prove all too brittle.

DARK STRATEGIC DREAMING

The way a country prepares for war, the assessment it makes of possible threats, is a deeply human process, prone to bias and instinct. It begins in the imagination. In his memoirs, Sir Arthur Tange, Australia's longest-serving and most consequential defence secretary, noted that:

> Unlike most areas of Commonwealth Government activity, defence and foreign policy have a constituency which is founded not so much on material and definable interests as on memories, inherited convictions about friends and likely enemies, along with associated fears and attachments, and some historical myths. Some memories and old faiths lose relevance because of radical change in weapons and surveillance technology; or because Australia's geopolitical environment has changed in directions not shared by the countries who have been our familiar friends and allies. But, on my observation of politics at work, it becomes difficult – particularly on the conservative side of politics – to change defence priorities rooted in the past.

Near the end of summer in 2006, Prime Minister John Howard sought to break foreign-policy thinking out of two opposing paradigms: should Australians seek to defend their geography or their values? He offered a vision of Australia's place in the world, at "a unique intersection of history, geography, culture and economic circumstance." "Australia is a liberal democracy with global political and economic interests and a proud history of defending freedom against its enemies," Howard intoned. "We do not have to smother or apologise for our place in the Western political tradition in order to build our relationships in Asia or in any other part of the world."

But there are tensions to be resolved in any imagining of Australia's role that aims at global reach, and to protect values as well as territory. Brendan Sargeant, now the second-most senior civilian defence leader in Australia, wrote not long after Howard gave his address:

> The Australian landscape is our destiny and thus the final reference point for the deep legitimacy of our defence strategy, and ultimately, of our deployments, no matter where our soldiers might be or the stated reasons why they are there. No war or deployment can be understood without understanding how it interacts with anxieties about our identity.

The period of the East Timor campaign of 1999 was perhaps the closest Australia has come to resolving the tensions inherent in how it imagines the world and our place in it. It was a popular military campaign, close to home, in support of our values, with clear political goals. It was endorsed by the United Nations and positioned Australia as both regional leader and neighbourly saviour. Above all, it concluded successfully. The public, the national security establishment and the political leadership were substantially aligned.

But now there is a gulf between the imagined world of Australia's national security establishment and the imagined world of the Australian public. For much of the Australian public, Australia's strategic environment has become somewhat safer. War has largely ceased to be a threat, and when it does occur, it is a distant and discretionary activity. Something to be lamented, but also ignored, as we continue on with our lives.

With the release of the 2016 Defence White Paper, though, the imagined future world of our defence planners and political leaders is beginning to show itself. This future world has an Asia where richer nations divert their wealth into funding more powerful militaries armed with ever more precise, long-range and lethal systems. Where gangs and terrorist groups communicate securely, and cheaply acquire weapons and technology that would once have been confined to special forces. Where renewed territorial friction across the globe, from Europe through the Middle East to the South China Sea, is fuelled by hyperactive nationalism and the instantaneous flow of information and disinformation alike. Where a major power like Russia has shown with its actions in Ukraine that brutal geopolitics and war for conquest remain a threat. Where the United States is engaged in a prolonged contest with China that extends across every domain – from space to commerce. And where interests and objectives overlap in newly complex ways.

Such imaginings of Australia and the world are darkening by the day, outracing the public imagination and leaving unaddressed the legitimacy of plans to build the most advanced and complex defence force Australia has ever seen.

In the halls of the defence headquarters clustered by Canberra's Lake Burley Griffin, on bases spread from Perth to Puckapunyal, amid the Gold Coast hinterland, in shipyards and on the high seas, and in the clean rooms of advanced factories in northern Adelaide, a new ADF is being built. Across the Commonwealth the effort is consuming the attentions of more than 100,000 employees; it is exercising Australia's diplomatic corps, stretching the decision-making capabilities of the federal government, vexing the most senior leaders in Canberra. It is an effort focused on the first priority of any elected body: how to keep citizens and interests safe from harm? How to prepare for the possibility of conflict without precipitating it?

The 2016 Defence White Paper commits Australia to investing more than $450 billion in defence in the next decade. The current annual defence budget of $32 billion – the thirteenth-largest in the world – will rise to $59 billion in 2025–26. Though it remains just 6 per cent of Commonwealth expenditure, it is a colossal amount of money by any measure. Some of the projects exist on a scale that defies everyday comprehension. One of them, the complex effort to design and build a new and greatly expanded fleet of submarines, could cost more than $50 billion – perhaps the largest line item of expenditure by a government in our lifetimes. To put the complexity of this project in some perspective, consider that it takes about 50,000 hours and 100,000 parts to build a large modern passenger jet. On one estimate, building a new submarine takes 2.5 million hours and 500,000 parts. Australia plans to build twelve of the largest conventional submarines in the world. Completing this project, as well as the other ship-building projects underway, will require the relocation of hundreds if not thousands of naval engineers and experts. These projects will outlast governments and run for decades. Australia will be relying on some of this equipment when I become a grandparent.

Behind the boom in defence construction, training and preparation is a vision of what kind of ADF will be needed to underpin security in the future. Since 2000, defence white papers have been completed every four years or so, updating assessments of global security, communicating the government's political priorities, and amending the military as necessary. The process has a bias towards very incremental change: militaries rightly tend to be conservative and rarely reinvent themselves from one white paper to the next. In Australia's case, the structure of the Australian Defence Force has remained relatively stable since the era of Menzies.

Australia has a small but sophisticated army, able to deploy offshore in up to brigade strength (3000 to 4000 troops) and conduct operations ranging from lower-intensity peacekeeping and humanitarian relief all the way through to combat. The army also maintains a small but potent special forces, able to conduct counter-terrorism domestically and a range of niche operations abroad, and to provide highly skilled fighters for international missions.

Australia's navy, too, is small but sophisticated. Our submarines patrol Australia's sea-lanes, conduct surveillance that warns of any threat, and can defeat anyone who might seek to interfere with Australia-bound shipping or harass Australian ports. The navy regularly performs constabulary tasks: boarding ships, conducting patrols, monitoring congested waterways. But it is a true blue-water navy as well, able to project across the globe and contribute to naval operations, including through offensive action. And the navy has supported Australia's major conflicts: ferrying troops, vehicles and stores to diverse locations, providing floating command centres for operations in places such as Bougainville and the Solomon Islands.

The air force has a highly sophisticated fleet of fighter jets, able to defend Australian territory or be deployed to foreign airfields to conduct limited strikes against enemy targets or in support of troops fighting on the ground. A powerful fleet of surveillance aircraft has been pivotal to the ADF since the 1960s, sweeping surrounding seas and providing eyes on the Indian and Pacific Oceans, South China Sea and South West Pacific. And the air force has long maintained planes able to move forces around the region, and more recently around the world.

This is what has come to be known as the "balanced force," able to do a little of all the tasks that might come its way, but sufficiently under-strength not to be able to operate in large numbers for any indefinite period of time. To know why, it helps to understand what some in the military call "mathematactics." Maintaining a unit in the field soon exhausts both people and equipment. For that reason, defence planners often work on a rule of threes. Keeping one submarine deployed means having another at home in maintenance, and a third working up the skills and procedures necessary to head out on operations next. So, crudely, to determine the resources the ADF can apply to any problem likely to last longer than a few weeks, divide what you see by three. Australia maintains three army brigades centred on Townsville, Darwin and Brisbane. In reality, only one of these can be committed to military operations at a time. For much of the past decade, through Iraq and Afghanistan, the Australian Defence Force has aspired to be able to deploy a brigade to a major operation, as well as maintaining another smaller unit (a battalion of up to 1000 personnel) for a separate contingency. The reality is that when it has been able to match this aspiration, it has been a very temporary and brittle state of affairs. So it is significant that the "Australian Defence Force 2030" plans to expand the balanced force in all directions.

This will include: a new amphibious force centred on two helicopter carriers, a new fleet of three air warfare destroyers, a doubled submarine fleet, a more capable special forces with global reach, a larger army equipped with more potent weapons, and an air force with long-range maritime reconnaissance drones and high-endurance patrol aircraft able to sweep the oceans. Defence is also investing billions in what it terms "decision-making superiority": new sensors (in the air, on the ground, in space, underwater and in the cyber domain) as well as systems that will boost our ability to see any future conflict or crisis coming from a long way off. This includes enhancements to the Jindalee over-the-horizon radar system that scans into Asia, new surveillance satellite constellations, and a massive increase of 1200 personnel in defence intelligence. Most importantly, though, a quarter of the increased defence funding the 2016 Defence White Paper promises for the next decade will go towards what are known as "force enablers": logistics, intelligence, command-and-control linkages. This is the largely unseen mortar bonding the defence force together.

The 2016 Defence White Paper does not see major conflict in our region as likely, but it clearly has made the judgment that such conflict is possible. That much is communicated by efforts to boost stocks and develop defence infrastructure in northern Australia. One example is particularly telling: hidden behind mountains in the upper Hunter Valley of New South Wales is a defence facility that stockpiles munitions for use in wartime: both the stockpile and the facility itself are being expanded. For years Australia has had bare bases in our north from which aircraft might operate, but never the fuel distribution systems to sustain them in the event of conflict. Now Defence plans to upgrade infrastructure and supply in those locations and in other places as remote as Australia's Indian Ocean Cocos Island territory. Finally, although in past decades Defence has sought to maintain squadrons of advanced fighter jets to guard against regional threats, it has never developed the air defence systems in our northern cities necessary to support this. Now the latest defence white paper talks about the acquisition of radars and missiles that might contribute to an integrated air defence system across our skies.

In tandem with these reforms, Defence is reforming the way it makes strategy, and committing the highest levels of funding ever to develop regional networks of liaison officers with advanced language skills. The command structure of the Australian Defence Force is being overhauled to clarify how the chief of the defence force directs forces during a time of conflict. Support for these reforms, among those politicians focused on them, has been surprisingly bipartisan. Among those thinking this way are two Labor MPs, Clare O'Neil and Tim Watts, who conclude in their recent book, Two Futures, that "the end of stable and benign American military hegemony in our region will significantly increase the strategic demands on our defence forces. The escalating strategic risks in our region demand a commensurate increase in our defence capabilities: both in raw funding and in our intellectual capacity to debate defence questions as a nation." Too often, they argue, "defence policy has been left to ideologues and technocrats, and the broad centre that gives good policy-making ballast is empty. This leaves our defence policy dangerously unmoored."

The build-up of the Australian Defence Force is well underway; the government has backed up its judgment that war could be a possibility within the next two decades with many billions of dollars. But Australians have barely begun to think through the consequences of all this, nor thought seriously about the circumstances that might bring our nation to the point of conflict.

THE DECISION

Over time, more and more power has accrued to the Australian prime minister. This trend is particularly apparent in the case of decisions to go to war. The Australian constitution, like the British, reserves for the crown the power to declare war, and apportions this responsibility to the governor-general. The last time Australia formally declared war, seventy years ago, it was the governor-general who did so. But in practice, since World War II it has been prime ministers who have effectively exercised the powers of commander-in-chief, and largely free of any formal legislative requirement for consultation or contestability.

When the ADF was committed to military action in Iraq in both 1991 and 2003, the governor-general was notified after the decision had been made, rather than consulted as part of the decision-making process. Without any requirement to ratify military deployments through parliament, prime ministers have chosen to announce through the press that the country is joining hostilities or commencing military action. On most occasions, but not all, parliamentary discussion of the deployment has taken place after this. When Bob Hawke sent a naval taskforce in 1991 to join the conflict in the Persian Gulf, he specifically recalled parliament to discuss the deployment. When Howard committed Australia to return to Iraq in 2003, he allowed for an extensive debate in the parliament lasting several days. But in most cases where the parliament has debated war, there has been no vote on a motion for or against the deployment. Instead, the defence minister or prime minister reads a statement (often echoing what has been briefed to the media), and a vote is taken to note the statement. In this way, few of the specifics of military objectives or strategy receive an airing. Some deployments have taken place without any parliamentary debate whatsoever, such as the 2001 contribution to the campaign in Afghanistan and Australia's deployment to Somalia in 1993. There are surprisingly few steps that a prime minister wanting to deploy the Australian military on combat operations must take.

How then does a prime minister embark on a decision for military action? In recent history there have been three avenues of approach. The first is a request by the United Nations for support, such as Australia received for East Timor in May 1999 or Cambodia in 1995. The second is a request that Australia might receive, or reasonably expect to receive, from an ally or partner, often the United States, as in the case of Iraq in 2003 or Afghanistan in 2001. Finally, there are situations in which Australia might independently decide to initiate action, such as in the Solomon Islands conflict of the early 2000s, the Fijian coup of 1987 or the MH17 crash of 2014. The process is convoluted, and may involve aspects of all three approaches. Peter Reith, defence minister during the Afghanistan deployment in 2001, illuminated some of these complexities in his recent memoir, The Reith Papers, sketching how a request for Australian troops from President George W. Bush was carefully calibrated and constructed over weeks. First, discussions took place between Minister for Foreign Affairs Downer and the US secretary of state, Colin Powell. Then there ensued a period in which it was not clear if a formal US request would be forthcoming. "They don't want to 'request' our military forces because then the others in the coalition will also want requests that the US doesn't want to make . . . we'll not deploy until Howard has had a call from George W. Bush. Whether it's a request or not is not really the issue – but he has to ring first." A month later, simultaneous formal requests for specific military support from the US military and state department were delivered to Australian officials.

It is a kabuki dance of sorts: official statements are made that no request has been issued, while at the bureaucratic level careful effort goes into communicating how and when one might be received. The mechanics of the request are important – whether it comes through military channels, by ambassadors or through the personal interaction of leaders. It is also a supremely political process, concerned with optics for international and domestic audiences, and open to miscalculation and even mischief. On at least one recent occasion, it is alleged that a request from the United States was procured purely to meet Australian domestic political objectives. But how to respond to a request, or to a brewing crisis, is entirely the prerogative of the prime minister. Some PMs have made the decision largely alone, bringing it to the National Security Committee of Cabinet as a fully formed idea ready to be rubber-stamped. Others have closely engaged small groups of ministers as confidants to explore options. Rarely is the decision brought to cabinet by the defence minister alone. All too often, defence ministers have been relegated to the role of "Minister Assisting the Prime Minister for Defence."

It is important, then, to ask how well-equipped recent prime ministers have been to assess international crises, determine political objectives and craft military strategies in pursuit of them. And the same question ought to be asked of the National Security Committee members. (The NSC currently consists of the deputy prime minister, the treasurer, the foreign minister, the attorney-general, the defence minister and the cabinet secretary, with support from defence and intelligence chiefs.) Very few prime ministers and National Security Committee members come to the role with an understanding of military matters, and other than on the job there are few places they can acquire this. Australian politicians are less likely to have had experience in the military, or working on military issues, than their counterparts in other countries. Of course, prime ministers rely on networks of personal advisers, their departments and the military in the formulation of strategy and oversight of the military options presented to them. But the networks of trained strategic analysts with political acumen are thin among staffers and even in departments. The defence department has a handful of excellent strategists, but a prime minister needs to be able to assess independently the recommendations he or she is receiving from defence. In his excellent book *Supreme Command*, Eliot Cohen traces how four leaders – Lincoln, Clemenceau, Churchill and Ben-Gurion – gave strategic direction to their militaries. Chief among the qualities required are the ability to scrutinise, evaluate and if necessary fire generals, to understand the issues at the heart of military debates, to maintain a vision and prod military leaders towards it when necessary, and to challenge received military opinion. Or, as Lawrence Freedman has put it, "pick your generals wisely, treat none as indispensable, and immerse yourself in the details of their trade. Learn about new technologies and logistical problems, follow debates on tactics, read intelligence reports, and reflect on past military experience."

Strategic direction starts at the top and is inherently political – it must be, for only elected politicians have the mandate to determine the military action that the public will deem legitimate and which will best serve the polity. But for many of the wars Australia has fought in the past decade, the strategic direction given by our political leaders to our defence chiefs has been remarkably episodic. One former chief of army, Peter Leahy, describes it as "set-and-forget" strategy: commit to the war, then leave Washington or the Australian military to fill in the blanks where the strategy should be. A recent damning ADF review looked at the strategic problems Australia has experienced while fighting this past decade. It consulted a distinguished list of interviewees, military and civilian. Two of the latter concluded that "policy formulated to guide the development of strategy was weak or missing," that politicians did not always act in a strategic manner – "For a number the strategic end state was not clear" – and that strategic decision-making lacked discipline and form. The problem extended to the military's own planning. Nowhere in the Australian Defence Organisation was there a body tasked with developing "just in case" strategic planning, nor was this being done by other government agencies. Strategy was left to be made reactively, by one man or woman.

This concentration of war powers in the hands of the prime minister, when combined with institutional shortcomings, creates potential problems in decision-making that could cost lives. There are very few checks and balances. Australia's parliament has a particularly feeble system of review and accountability for military operations and strategic decisions, there are no procedures to determine the difference between political and military strategy, and in any event the military is culturally and institutionally muzzled from speaking on issues to do with the deployment of troops. The public is barely a check on prime ministerial authority to make decisions on war either. In a report completed for the Department of Defence, Ian McAllister noted a "rally 'round the flag effect": once a decision to deploy military force is made, public support will swing behind the government – at least for the initial phase of the campaign. The danger of the current system is that the main checks on the power of the prime minister to take Australia to war are his or her own intellect and character.

*

Although he had little direct experience of the military before becoming prime minister, Tony Abbott developed a deep fascination for it in office. "Every man thinks meanly of himself for not having been a soldier," he was fond of saying, quoting Samuel Johnson. Greeting troops at military bases, he would tell them, "If I can't serve with you, I can at least sweat with you." Military imagery laced the titles of his books. It permeated his conception of Australian nationalism and history: "remember the Western Front, not just for its carnage, but also for Australia's moment on the stage of history," he implored an Anzac Day gathering in 2014. And once in office, the military preoccupied him.

All the ingredients were there for Abbott's stewardship of the defence forces to be a successful one. Before taking office he made a considered speech to the national RSL in which he pledged to examine Australia's defence forces and strategic environment through a new white paper, and gave a commitment to fund defence adequately. His staff were experienced in foreign policy, his senior adviser for national security a practitioner with deep connections in Canberra and the United States and a sophisticated understanding of Asia. During Abbott's first year in office, Defence chiefs set aside whole weekends for the prime minister and his staff to do deep dives into issues like defence procurement. His initial reflections on Australian power were modest: in an interview with the *Sydney Morning Herald*'s Peter Hartcher he reflected that Australia had "concerns wherever bad things are happening, but we don't necessarily have any significant influence or capacity to offer anything other than well-intentioned advice." But when tested by three international crises during 2014, a more reactive and muscular commander-in-chief emerged.

In a little over six months, driven by Abbott's unilateral instincts, the Australian government nearly committed troops to conflicts on three continents, and countenanced the riskiest of missions, including one arrayed against a global military power. The first hint of this new approach to the use of military force came after 276 Nigerian schoolgirls were kidnapped by the terrorist group Boko Haram in April 2014, an incident that attracted global attention and calls for the United States and United Kingdom to intervene. In the weeks afterwards, journalists were briefed that Australia's special forces were on standby, ready to join efforts to track down and confront the kidnappers. This was an expansive and dangerous task for Australia to perform in a country with which our military had little familiarity and where our country had few direct interests. But this was only the start.

Just after midnight Australian time on 17 July 2014, Malaysian Airlines flight MH17 failed to respond to calls from Rostov-on-Don air control and vanished from its flight path between Amsterdam and Kuala Lumpur. That morning's news reported 238 bodies lying in a burnt field near the city of Donetsk in Eastern Ukraine, including thirty-eight Australians: victims of an apparent missile hit. The culprits were either the Ukrainians or the Russian-backed separatists – or one of them trying to make it look like the other. That morning I jotted down thoughts for a Lowy Institute blog post, including the bones of a likely Australian response. A multinational air-crash investigation would be necessary, no easy feat in a war-torn region washed back and forth by the Ukrainian military and the separatists of the self-declared republic of Donetsk. Not to mention their mysterious supporters, the irregular but superbly equipped militia known as the "little green men," who were believed to have been trained by Russian advisers. Australia would want to contribute, and the leader of our effort would require an understanding of the military and the protocols of international aviation, and some sort of relationship with the Malaysian government. Only one name sprang to mind: Angus Houston, former chief of the defence force, chair of Airservices Australia, and recently engaged in the search for the missing Malaysian Airlines flight MH370.

After considering the sensitivities of operating in a war zone and within the shadow of the border of a faded superpower with one of the world's largest conventional militaries, I concluded that the presence of the military would be counter-productive. This mission would be best left to federal police and diplomats, preferably unarmed to emphasise the non-military forensic nature of their work. If the situation was unstable enough to require means of immediate self-defence, the AFP should carry side-arms. As an afterthought, I forwarded my blog post to a friend working in the national security field. He replied almost straightaway to let me know he was thinking along the same lines. But Prime Minister Tony Abbott was thinking on a grander scale.

Again, the first instinct was to deploy Australia's special forces; nearly 200 were eventually sent to Europe to support the MH17 recovery operations, staging from bases in the United Kingdom and the Netherlands to provide close support to investigators and backup for further crisis or contingency. Later in 2014, it would be reported that Abbott had considered deploying up to a battalion, or 1000 troops, to Eastern Ukraine in the days after the plane was shot down. As the *Australian* revealed, "Australia's leading military planners . . . argued against that proposal, telling Mr Abbott there were serious problems with the plan: Australian soldiers would not be able to speak either Ukrainian or Russian, and the Australian troops would have difficulty distinguishing between Ukrainians and Russian militia." Beyond these concerns, the response of Russia to having an armed formation from a NATO partner country dropped near a sensitive border was a major issue. The potential for harm to Australian troops was all too real. The logic of deploying large numbers of troops into an active war zone alongside the border of a major global military power was entirely shaky.

In fact, I have since learnt, military planners worked up options for Abbott that involved deploying up to a brigade's worth of troops to Eastern Ukraine, a formation of as many as 3000 troops. A brigade-sized deployment would have been Australia's largest military deployment since the East Timor crisis of 1999, and maintaining it would have consumed the bulk of the Australian Army. As Abbott himself later concluded, "Placing substantial numbers of Australian troops within twenty-five miles of a hostile Russian army was a scenario that no one had ever before contemplated." Further curious military proposals were floated by staff from the prime minister's office: one of them – to commit uniformed Australian military logistics personnel to help the Ukrainians improve their own systems – seemed to ignore that this would make them legitimate targets for separatists fighting in Eastern Ukraine. Planning for these military options consumed Australia's intelligence agencies. The National Security Committee of Cabinet met every day for more than three weeks, and staff and agencies produced a frenzied stream of briefings on Ukraine, Russia and the intentions of Vladimir Putin.

In August 2014 Australia's attentions swung from Ukraine to the security crisis in Iraq, where ISIS was consolidating its hold on Mosul, as well as marauding against towns near Mount Sinjar. Here, too, Abbott mused on deploying large numbers of Australian troops. According to one report, he considered unilaterally sending an Australian brigade to northern Iraq. As it was, Australia sent 600 personnel, again leading with more than 100 special-forces personnel who came directly from the MH17 mission in Europe. Asked to outline the mission for the 600, Abbott replied, "Our mission is to work for the betterment of mankind." I assumed there would be more strategic detail in the directives issued to the ADF to carry out Operation Accordion (as the mission in Iraq became known), but this mission appeared to be a "set-and-forget" mission too, like Afghanistan. For months after Australian forces deployed, there was no strategic direction connecting the tactical military tasks they were performing with the overall political objective. Instead, military staff within the department's

Russell Headquarters drafted strategic directives to themselves, then sent them across the lake to be endorsed.

An article by Simon Benson, who had unusually detailed access to National Security Committee and intelligence developments during Abbott's leadership, spelled out the essence of the prime minister's approach to the three crises of Nigeria, Iraq and Ukraine. Under the headline "Australia Muscling up as a Middle Power," it described Abbott's approach, using a series of telling words and phrases: "muscle," "provocative," "assertive," "committed," "a serious player," "firm," "hawkish," "instinctive," "had not flinched." A clear picture emerges of the world leader Abbott intended to be. His policy responses "derived from an unwavering moral position," and he was ready to call out evil where it appeared in the world. A man of action, he was inspired by Churchill, whose books he read constantly and whose bust gazed down on him in the prime minister's office at Parliament House.

This model of global activism was based on three principles. First, Abbott judged that to have credibility as a middle power, to be a voice of influence on international issues, Australia needed to have skin in the game and troops committed. Second, responses to security crises should be led by values. Standing by while the world burned was immoral and unacceptable. And third, Abbott calculated that the best way to encourage the United States to retain an active role in world affairs was for Australia to lead by example: as an ally encouraging, reassuring and perhaps even occasionally shaming the US into taking action.

But his use of the military to achieve these ends was problematic – chaotic, even. He pushed Australia's small defence force and decision-making structures to their limit, engaged as they were in deliberating troop contributions on three continents (as well as fulfilling existing responsibilities on UN missions, in Afghanistan and closer to Australia). He overcommitted Australia's special forces and strategic airlift to operations in areas of less strategic value to Australia, leaving little reserve should crises arise closer to home. His grand aspirations for the ADF in the world could have exposed Australian troops to substantial danger in pursuit of lofty objectives misaligned with national interests.

Abbott's stewardship of the ADF presents the clearest case in recent times of a prime minister struggling to grasp the limits of Australian military power. As much as overreach, Abbott's thinking also reflects the flaws in Australia's military model of the last decade. Ours have been niche, discrete, tactical contributions, particularly of special forces, made to assist US coalitions. That model may no longer be appropriate for a world of strategic rivalry among major powers. In a world in which the United States and China are in prolonged competition, the decisions Australia makes on the alliance and the use of the nation's military will be more complex, more deliberate, and involve combinations of responses rather than just the dispatch of one or two units. A better system for deciding to go to war will be needed – one that fosters long-term strategy, that can manage simultaneous crises, and in which prime ministers are well advised, but also have their power balanced.

*

In their own way, prime ministers Howard, Gillard and Rudd each tinkered with Australia's system for going to war. Howard began to build the Department of the Prime Minister and Cabinet as a place where policy could be coordinated, and brought across General Angus Campbell to the Office of National Security, where he was to provide advice independent to that of the military. Gillard launched a national security strategy that for the first time aligned the goals and budgets of disparate agencies and departments. Better coordination was her priority – "My message to the community is if you see a silo, dig it up" – but it came with little additional funding, the judgment that the age of terrorism was over, and a defence white paper that declared all was better in the world than the government had thought.

It was Rudd who turbocharged the effort. In 2008 he appointed Australia's first official national security adviser, Duncan Lewis, a former general who set about drafting the country's first national security statement. By this time, the Department of Foreign Affairs and Trade (DFAT), the traditional coordinator of international policy, was anaemic and lacked both the skills and people to drive a long-term security strategy and scrutinise the defence department. Rudd believed new international risks required a more coordinated approach, and he meant everything from the security threats resulting from climate change to the Taliban fighting against Australians in Afghanistan. Rudd launched a National Security College at the Australian National University to bring in officials from across government and sharpen their skills. New cabinet committees were formed, as well as bodies to coordinate intelligence-gathering and emergency and counter-terrorism responses. An assessment of these reforms by the Australian Strategic Policy Institute concluded that they were in step with efforts in the United Kingdom and the United States to improve decision-making after the Iraq disaster.

The new structure was a promising start, but in time it fell victim to Rudd's personal style of leadership: intense, exhausting, overly ambitious and ultimately short-term. The national security adviser was asked to range across too many issues, from bushfires in Victoria to refugee policy and matters of war. An increasing number of policy matters were "securitised" – that is, considered as a security issue. At the same time, authority was centralised. The Department of the Prime Minister and Cabinet, in the words of one DFAT assistant secretary, was "overwhelmed supporting Rudd's foreign policy activities, particularly his travel," and DFAT itself was marginalised. A cable from America's embassy in Canberra, obtained by WikiLeaks, concluded: "The PM's office tends to respond to the media cycle and the next event on the schedule and cannot focus on longer-term policy development."

The first step in fixing the way we go to war is to revisit the efforts of Rudd, Gillard and Howard, with a view to what they got right and wrong. At present, the formulation of independent national security advice for the prime minister is a somewhat haphazard process – at the highest levels it lacks institutional rigour and continuity. No one is formulating long-term strategy for the government, or conducting the deep thinking necessary for a world in which competition between our friends and allies is the new normal. DFAT has largely vacated this role, and in its place the Department of Defence has all too often been solipsistically crafting its own strategic direction.

This is not a role for Prime Minister and Cabinet, focused as it is on the prime minister's immediate needs and the day-to-day coordination of departments and agencies. Rather, what is needed is a new national security council headed by a national security adviser with a role and powers detailed in legislation.

There are difficulties with having a somewhat independent adviser and secretariat within the Westminster system. But the United Kingdom has found a way: in 2005 it created a new national security council with a chief who can be called before parliament (although not in the same way as a minister or departmental secretary). A national security council would house the best and brightest strategic thinkers so that they can work with – and critique – each other and link with partners abroad. It would do more to connect Australia's bifurcated discussions of economics and security. Of course, building such an institution and its culture is a complex task, requiring an un-Rudd-like patience. Finding the right national security adviser will also be difficult. Too strong, and they hamper the ability of the prime minister and cabinet to exercise their democratic mandate, or else sideline the defence chiefs. Too weak and they don't provide enough contestability to balance the advice provided by the military.

To restore public trust in the decision to go to war, better democratic accountability is also essential. This is not just about giving parliament a vote on military deployments – after all, a prime minister will always command the approval of the lower house of parliament. Instead, democratic accountability means developing a system capable of exercising genuine oversight of the national security agencies and departments, particularly Defence. At the moment that oversight takes place in a few ways: through overly adversarial and hasty questioning at Senate estimates, abridged discussion in the lower house when prime ministers and their cabinets deign to allow discussion of national security or defence issues, and in the committee system.

Here it is telling to compare Australia's parliamentary committees for defence and national security with their counterparts in Canada and the United Kingdom. By contrast, Australia's oversight of national security is underdone and weak: one joint standing committee covers foreign affairs, defence and trade in toto. (A separate joint committee was established to cover intelligence and domestic security after the Hope royal commission into intelligence in the 1980s.) It is extraordinary that so little infrastructure is dedicated to parsing the issues of war. The National Disability Insurance Scheme, on which the government spends $15 billion each year, has an entire committee dedicated to its oversight. The national security apparatus, which accounts for more than 100,000 commonwealth employees and will soon absorb more than $45 billion each year, is entirely underscrutinised, and it shows. If one scans the list of issues examined, they pale by contrast with the omissions, which include the strategy underpinning the acquisition of Australia's submarines, defence white papers, military education and defence diplomacy.

The next parliament needs committees dedicated to assessing each of the ADF, the Department of Defence, national strategy and foreign affairs. This expanded committee system will require trained staff and political advisers with the necessary experience and judgment to grapple with the world of strategy and the opaque language of war – skills that are currently in short supply. The problem extends to the military itself. Ours is a military that gives priority to tactical rather than strategic excellence, and in which the ability to do battle in the realm of ideas has been more of a liability than an asset. That is starting to change, but only slowly. Our military colleges are not yet universities for the study of war and our universities still view war as a morally tainted activity. Furthermore, when so much defence decision-making is based on classified assessments and considerations routinely unavailable to members of the Opposition, there is a role for a body that can equip parliamentarians to discuss national security policy. For these reasons, it might prove necessary to create a parliamentary defence office, which seeks to improve the security debate in the same way as the recently established Parliamentary Budget Office has in the area of economics.

The need for full parliamentary approval before any substantial military action by the prime minister would inhibit an effective response to a crisis, and successive prime ministers have rightly resisted this. But there is a compelling case for parliament to review whether a military deployment is in the national interest within a period of, say, ninety days. Here we have a model in the way parliament deals with foreign treaties. Of course it is the role of the executive to sign treaties with other countries, and in the past it was entirely up to the foreign minister to present these treaties to the parliament for domestic legislation. But in 2005 reforms were introduced which require a new joint committee on treaties to prepare a statement on whether a treaty is in the national interest or not, and table it before the parliament. A similar system could be applied to the decision to go to war.

When should Australia go to war? The more we can think through the circumstances in which this question might arise, the less likely we will be to err in our calculations. Here are ten questions to be asked the next time our leaders want to commit Australian forces:

- Are our vital national interests threatened?
- Is there a clear political objective?
- Are our military aims linked to this political objective?
- Can the case be made to the Australian people that this campaign is in their interests, and can their support for the campaign be sustained through casualties and setbacks?
- Do we understand the costs – to the country, to civilian victims, to the enemy and to our veterans?
- What new dangers might this campaign cause?

- What proportion of the Australian Defence Force will it commit?
- What options will close to us if we take this action, and if we don't?
- Will the Opposition remain committed, should it form government?
- How does this end?

TOMORROW, WHEN THE WAR BEGAN ...

Since returning from Afghanistan and leaving the army I've spent Anzac Day most years with fellow veterans by the bay at Bondi. Our dawn service ends as the sun rises, with an injunction to the thousand-strong crowd to turn to face the Pacific Ocean. Ever since this place was a colony, a fledgling outpost on the far side of the earth, Sydneysiders have been thinking about what might come to threaten us from across the sea. In the nineteenth century, when colonial engineers were constructing the last Martello tower of the British Empire at Fort Denison, Australia's strategic environment was easily distilled in a single image: two broad red arrows thrusting their way into Sydney Harbour and Botany Bay, bringing threats from the outside world.

Listening to the reveille by the sea, I have often wondered how an enemy appearing at Bondi Beach might be met, and what kind of fight Australians might bring to them. This year, *Tomorrow, When the War Began*, the television adaptation of the popular series of children's books, is being screened. There is something primal in this dreaming of young Australians rallying to a crisis, forging a community at a time of adversity and fighting an invading army as they would a summer bushfire. They answer the call much as their grandparents' and great-grandparents' generations did when forced unprepared from civilian life into the global conflicts of World Wars I and II. But enemy forces, let alone threats to Australia's sovereign interests, are not likely to land at Bondi telegraphing their intent. Limiting our imagination of threat in this way is like failing to heed bushfire warnings until the flames are licking the veranda. The harder questions are out there beyond the surf, where tracing the boundaries of our interests and values has become much harder.

Some of us will support any decision by the government to take us to war, and some of us will never accept the deployment of military force as a legitimate activity of government. In the middle, though, is the mass of us seldom provoked to think about war, but who, infused with stories of Gallipoli and Iraq, harbour a hidden instinct for splendid isolation. Permit me the imprecision of grafting psychological theory onto such an abstract thing as our national thinking on war. In a time of crisis, when there are numerous witnesses to an event, a collective diffusion of responsibility can occur, known as the bystander effect. A decision is taken not to become involved, but it is a decision all the same. It seems to me that many Australians want to default to the role of bystander, particularly when it comes to the changing power balances in Asia, and the role of the United States. Some are bystanders because they mistakenly think our allies are big enough to fight on their own. Some think our allies are ugly, continually rushing to fight and shed blood, sowing little more than mayhem. Some bystanders, perhaps, are afraid of what it might mean to intervene, concerned for how the danger to us might increase, judging that we might find peace as a gentle democracy, trading and travelling but never fighting. Some bystanders believe we are strong enough and distant enough to be insulated from the evils of the world. But all of these bystanders are making the same unconscious decision: to turn away from the problems of the world, to make them someone else's responsibility. To put that choice in David Morrison's familiar terms: the standard you walk past is the standard you accept.

For most of our history we have allowed others to set the international standards for conflict and security. Thresholds for war in 1914 and 1939 were set beyond our shores. In an internationalised, interconnected, federated and globalised world it is tempting to give over entire responsibility for those standards to the United Nations. But for all its virtues, the United Nations can sometimes be feeble and fractious, plagued by the same petty politics it aspires to overcome, and slow to respond to evil in the world. Most troublingly, it has struggled to grapple with security issues in Asia, particularly where its permanent powers are arrayed on opposing sides. We cannot rely solely on the United States to set the international standard, either. At its worst the US is fallible, distracted, introverted and proud. It can be a jealous power, blinded at times to pragmatic outcomes by its exceptionalism. Our understanding of the standards we wish to see in the world will be informed by both the United Nations and the United States, by our interactions with neighbours, and by events.

Read through the texts of Australian thinking on war in the past forty years and you will find many points at which commentators bemoan the more uncertain and complex future that awaits us. Australian defence and strategy experts are fond of writing of inflection points, shifts and epochal change in the security environment. But this time there are tangible markers that suggest we should give more thought to how our world is shifting. The decision to hew more closely to the United States and at the same time develop independent influence and authority in Asia has been endorsed by five political leaders with varying perspectives on the world and Australia's place in it. There seems little doubt that leaders of differing political persuasions, as well as the officials who work for them, have concluded that Australia needs a stronger insurance policy for a more uncertain and potentially troubled environment, one in which nations will jostle for advantage, core ideals and claims will be tested, and in which military force or the slightest threat of it will be a persistent tool of national interest.

I don't think Australia wants to be, can or should be a bystander to the complexities playing out around us. I don't think we want to be a lonely island, removed from the world and indifferent to its course. We are not a people that can live in splendid isolation: the hard reality is that we are entangled by the nature of the country we are and wish to become, not to speak of the standard of living we expect. But despite this, there is a dangerous naivety to our thinking, a blindness to the possibility that, despite all the effort and attention, diplomacy might fail, tragic mistakes might happen, and miscalculations might be made with the potential to harm us and our interests. More often than not, the signs of impending conflict will fall like cinders in a world filled with more noise and distraction than ever before. It will take our best and brightest minds to catch them as sparks before they flare.

Almost fifteen years after 9/11, the American essayist James Fallows lamented the way his nation would do anything for its military except take it seriously:

> Citizens notice when crime is going up, or school quality is going down, or the water is unsafe to drink, or when other public functions are not working as they should . . . Not enough citizens are made to notice when things go wrong, or right, with the military . . . Too much complacency regarding our military, and too weak a tragic imagination about the consequences if the next engagement goes wrong, have been part of Americans' willingness to wade into conflict after conflict, blithely assuming we would win.

Fallows argues for more public debate on the military, the effectiveness of its people and machines, and the ease with which it can be sent off to war. Difficult questions, but he concludes that "for democracies, messy debates are less damaging in the long run than letting important functions run on autopilot." Australia needs similar debates. At one of the national town hall–style meetings held during the development of the 2016 Defence White Paper, a participant said, "We need to be given a national interest explanation of what we are doing with the ADF and why." In a companion report to the white paper, members of the public made the case that "relations with the United States had become closer in recent years without thorough explanation or sufficient public debate." The messy debates need to begin with a frank, long-overdue discussion of the military and political strategy underpinning the recent tightening of the Australian and American military partnership. The talking points on the South China Sea and the US forces in Darwin will soon start to wear thin.

In the next decade a less predictable North Korea will continue to menace Asia with its growing number of nuclear weapons. The Middle East will remain combustible and fragile. The states of the Southwest Pacific will remain just barely governed, with tribal politics prone to spill over into violence. On our doorstep, Papua New Guinea teeters towards instability, with politicians battling the High Court, as well as chronic corruption and rampant social and health problems. The rivalry of the United States and China will continue to play out, as the US builds a denser network of allies and partners and China grasps every advantage it can, particularly in the South China Sea and Southeast Asia. The future offers no shortage of potential trouble spots. New problems may emerge in places like Thailand, where Australians cluster for work and play, and where a looming generational leadership transition must take place in an atmosphere thick with suspicion and distrust. Transnational criminal networks will develop new and sophisticated ways of operating, and the radical and violent will find willing and competent followers to commit terrorist acts.

In the military realm, technology is fast running ahead of policy. Not just in the space and cyber realms, but in the plethora of other dark machines being developed that are being adopted by countries and leaking to malicious groups the world over: swarming weaponised drones, underwater vessels able to drift near-permanently in oceans to intercept shipping and submarines, 4D-printed objects which can change shape and structure at a pre-set time to shift from an everyday object to a weapon, dizzying changes in biologics, nanoscience and materials.

We are not yet ready for all of this. Australia is far from powerless in this new world; both our military muscle and diplomatic voice can be considerable when brought to bear at the right time and in the right way. But one thing is certain: as the complexities of Asia play out, we will need to pull back from arenas where we have less unique leverage. That will likely mean making fewer military contributions in the Middle East, and more in Southeast Asia.

None of this is to say that we should be more warlike. Indeed, the most significant contribution an Australian commander-in-chief might make to an international crisis, whether from within the US alliance or among the voices of neighbours in our region, could be to decry military action. But to be prepared to fight the cancer of war, we must know it, discuss it, think the malady through to its worst outcomes, understand and chart the darkest of possibilities. We cannot just wish the evils of the world away. Looking for means to defuse building tensions and to counter rising nationalism and territorialism, as well as coolly assessing the judgments of our allies and friends, will be more important than ever. Thinking like hawks, while moving like doves. And there is no time to waste, because the building of a larger and more ambitious Australian Defence Force is well underway. We risk having a large defence force, but not the wisdom to use it properly.

When President Barack Obama was awarded the Nobel Peace Prize in 2009, he had pledged himself to ending the wars in Iraq and Afghanistan. In his acceptance speech, though, he noted the "difficult questions about the relationship between war and peace, and our effort to replace one with the other":

> In many countries there is a deep ambivalence about military action today, no matter what the cause . . . We must begin by acknowledging the hard truth: we will not eradicate violent conflict in our lifetimes. There will be times when nations – acting individually or in concert – will find the use of force not only necessary but morally justified . . . For make no mistake: evil does exist in the world . . . To say that force may sometimes be necessary is not a call to cynicism – it is a recognition of history; the imperfections of man and the limits of reason.

SOURCES

8   "provide a secure environment": John Howard, Press conference, 22 February 2005, http://pmtranscripts.dpmc.gov.au/release/transcript-21622/.

8   "heavy burden" and "This decision and this deployment": John Howard, *Hansard*, 7 March 2005, p. 37.

8   "Australia is not just": Alexander Downer, *Hansard*, 7 March 2005, p. 30.

9   "The Labor Opposition": Kim Beazley, quoting Ben Chifley, *Hansard*, 7 March 2005, p. 41.

14 "The greatest disaster in American foreign policy": Madeleine Albright, Discussion with former president Jimmy Carter on Middle East Peace Prospects, Carter Center, 12 February 2007.

18 "another war in Iraq": Christine Milne, *Hansard*, 30 September 2014, p. 7269.

21 "when she declared": Hillary Clinton, Remarks at press availability, Hanoi, Vietnam, 23 July 2010, www.state.gov/secretary/20092013clinton/rm/2010/07/145095.htm.

22 "If this scenario goes ahead": Malcolm Fraser, "Australia–US Relations in the 'Asian Century'", Asialink lecture series, 25 September 2012.

22 "an oral and policy assault" etc.: Paul Keating, The Keith Murdoch Oration, 14 November 2012.

22 "China has been a better friend": James Packer, Australia in China's Century Conference, 14 September 2012.

22–3 "physically repulsed by the thought" etc.: Kerry Stokes, Australia in China's Century Conference, 14 September 2012.

25 ""Pivot" is well short": Michael Pascoe, "Australia Shouldn't Pay Price for Pivot", *Sydney Morning Herald*, 18 April 2016.

28 "It is legitimate": Dennis Richardson, "Defence Secretary Dennis Richardson's Blamey Oration", *Sydney Morning Herald*, 28 May 2015.

32 "What appeals to me": Roger Hertog, quoted in Amy Dockser Marcus, "Where Policy Makers Are Born", *Wall Street Journal*, 20 September 2008.

34 "The Australian government": Michael Green, Peter Dean, Brendan Taylor & Zack Cooper, *The ANZUS Alliance in Ascending Asia*, Strategic and Defence Studies Centre, 2015.

38 "Unlike most areas": Arthur Tange, *Defence Policy-Making: A Close-Up View, 1950–1980 – A Personal Memoir*, ANU E-Press, 2008, p. 40.

38 "a unique intersection" etc.: John Howard, Address to the National Press Club, 25 January 2006.

39 "The Australian landscape": Brendan Sargeant, "Burning Bright: Defence Policy, Strategy and the Imagination", *Australian Army Journal*, vol. 3, no. 3, 2006, p. 79.

44	"the end of stable and benign" etc.: Clare O'Neil and Tim Watts, *Two Futures: Australia at a Critical Moment*, Text Publishing, 2015, pp. 189, 195.
46	"They don't want to": Peter Reith, *The Reith Papers*, Melbourne University Press, 2015.
48	"pick your generals wisely": Lawrence Freedman, "Calling the Shots: Should Politicians or Generals Run Our Wars?", *Foreign Affairs*, vol. 81, no. 5, 2002, p. 190.
48	"set-and-forget": Peter Leahy, quoted in David Wroe, "Australia Had 'No Strategy in Afghanistan' and Allies Are Struggling, Says Former Army Chief Peter Leahy", *Age*, 23 February 2016.
48	"policy formulated to": Noetic, *Strategic Command and Control Lessons – Scoping Study*, July 2013, p. 8, www.defence.gov.au/FOI/Docs/Disclosures/343_10_11_Document.pdf.
49	"rally 'round the flag effect:" Ian McAllister, Appendix 3, "Public Opinion in Australia Towards Defence and Security" in Department of Defence, *Guarding Against Uncertainty: Australian Attitudes to Defence*, Commonwealth of Australia, 2015, p. 130.
49	"Every man thinks": Tony Abbott, to me and others. More on Abbott's use of defence: www.regionalsecurity.org.au/resources/Documents/SC%2012-1%20Carr.pdf.
49	"remember the Western Front": Tony Abbott, commemorative address for Anzac Day Ceremony, 25 April 2014, www.awm.gov.au/talks-speeches/commemorative-address-2014-anzac-day-national-ceremony/
50	"concerns wherever bad things are happening": Peter Hartcher, *Adolescent Country: A Lowy Institute Paper*, Penguin, 2014, pp. 75–6.
51	"Australia's leading military planners": Paul Kelly, "Leader for a More Dangerous World", *Australian*, 13 August 2014.
52	"Placing substantial numbers": Tony Abbott, quoted in Paul Kelly, "Tony Abbott Fights for Legacy", *Australian*, 26 March 2016.
52	"Our mission is": Tony Abbott, ABC interview, 2 September 2014, www.abc.net.au/7.30/content/2014/s4079649.htm.
53	"Australia Muscling up", etc.: Simon Benson, "Australia Muscling up as Middle Power", *Daily Telegraph*, 5 September 2014.
54	"My message": Julia Gillard, National Security Address at the ANU National Security College, 23 January 2013, https://pmtranscripts.dpmc.gov.au/release/transcript-19005.
55	"overwhelmed supporting Rudd's" and "The PM's office": Wikileaks, 11 February 2009, https://wikileaks.org/plusd/cables/09CANBERRA138_a.html.
58–9	"ten questions": Adapted from Colin Powell's doctrine.
63	"Citizens notice" etc.: James Fallows, "The Tragedy of the American Military", *Atlantic*, January/February 2015.

63 "We need to be given" and "relations with the United States": Department of Defence, *Guarding Against Uncertainty*, pp. 6, 36.

65 "difficult questions": Barack Obama, Remarks by the President at the Acceptance of the Nobel Peace Prize, 10 December 2009, www.whitehouse.gov/the-press-office/remarks-president-acceptance-nobel-peace-prize.

BALANCING ACT | Correspondence

Clare O'Neil

One fascination of economics is watching how trends in thinking ebb and flow. In the 1970s economic nationalism reigned. By the 1990s you were an economic rationalist or an economic illiterate. During the global financial crisis we were all Keynesians.

Today, Australia's economy faces obvious, urgent problems that none of these approaches will help us solve. Australians are not getting better at thinking, building and creating fast enough. For many, wages are growing slowly or not at all, and living standards in Australia have not improved for five years. The mining construction boom is drawing to a close, and the global economy is dominated by uncertainty and unease.

The old thinking isn't working anymore, here or overseas. We're not merely observing our economy in transition; there is a transition underway in how we think about government's role in helping Australia out of the mire.

Enter George Megalogenis, whose essay offers a clear-sighted perspective on how the toxicity of politics is contributing to our economic malaise, and a thoughtful, evidence-based argument about stronger government intervention in infrastructure and cities policy in particular. *Balancing Act* is not, and is not meant to be, a coherent new philosophy of how government and the economy ought to interact.

Politics is suffering due to a lack of agreement on this point. Much of our current economic debate feels as if it has no anchor, no shared starting point. One minute the scourge is budget deficit, the next the tax mix, then the tax burden on the middle class, then on companies. While we debate tax policy as though it is the only economic issue that matters, economic problems of vast national importance are being largely ignored.

In searching for a new way to think about government's role in the economy, it's worth noting that what Megalogenis describes as the "open economy" model has been deeply rooted in the minds of Australian politicians and the public for almost thirty years. If the resident galah knew anything, it was that the best thing government could do for the economy was get out of the way. But suddenly, evidence is everywhere that the time for this idea has come and gone.

Today, there is broad recognition on both sides of politics that government shapes and influences our economy: it cannot avoid doing so. Government spending in Australia is 37 per cent of GDP. Some government interventions are very direct, such as removing support to the car industry, or signing a free-trade agreement that privileges one industry over another. Some are less direct: how much funding we provide to the CSIRO, how many young people we train in metallurgy or medical science, whether we build a new freight link in Penrith or Perth.

The bipartisan engagement on innovation policy demonstrates this shift in thinking. Today, it is accepted that innovation matters to economic growth, and that governments drive innovation through regulation, universities policy and other means, such as investment in science and research. This flies in the face of traditional economic thinking, but it has been adopted by Australian politicians with very little comment, because the evidence that it works is so strong.

The shift away from dogma is a global phenomenon. In Europe and the United States, economic decision-makers are busily enacting policies (for example, trying to drive growth by printing more money) which would have been sacrilegious a decade ago. There is global interest in the work on inequality of Thomas Piketty and organisations like the IMF and the OECD. All are arguing that without government intervention capitalist economies will create unequal societies, and that over time this will slow growth. Social policy is back in vogue, for economic reasons as much as any others.

Academic economics, too, is throwing off the shackles of textbook thinking. The exciting field of behavioural economics argues that some of the foundation principles of the science are, when tested in the real world, utterly wrong.

These shifts have a common thread: pragmatism over philosophy, real-world thinking over textbook, evidence over theory. We may not be looking at a new economic orthodoxy, but rather a shift away from orthodoxy altogether. The guiding principle for government intervention might therefore be this: governments should engage where the evidence shows they can make a difference.

If we used this thinking to build an economic agenda for the nation, I think we would find there is plenty for Australian governments to do that is urgent, obvious and the subject of wide consensus.

If we asked most decision-makers and economists what the evidence tells us matters most to Australia's prosperity, and what government can influence, I think they would agree on five big challenges. Our education system, so important to underpinning today's prosperous Australia, is fast falling behind that of our peers. The sluggish engagement with Asia by Australian business and governments is seeing other countries sweep up export and partnership opportunities that Australians have long regarded as fait accomplis. Climate change has become an undeniable reality, and the chance to become a global renewables powerhouse is slipping from our grasp. We are lagging behind in big infrastructure investments (broadband, public transport) with huge potential to drive growth. And there are concerns about whether Australia could weather another financial crisis, due to the growing debt of Australian governments and households.

Not everyone will agree on how to order these issues, and some will add one or two to the list. But any government looking for an economic agenda can find plenty to get on with here, purely on problems that virtually everyone agrees are critical.

Yet we spend disappointingly little time in politics talking about these, the most important economic issues facing our nation. Why this is so has plagued me since being elected to parliament almost three years ago. As a journalist, Megalogenis evidently finds it frustrating to comment on. As a politician, it can feel enraging to participate in.

One part of the problem that I see up close is that our political culture is addicted to conflict. Question Time, the centre stage of our democracy, is dominated by aggressive posturing and tit-for-tat point-scoring – an abominable way to conduct a deliberative process and, on many days, a total waste of time. Some politicians feel that focusing on areas of consensus is a missed opportunity to highlight political differences between the parties. From a policy perspective, this kind of thinking is starting to hurt Australia badly. And politically, I think it misreads the desires of the electorate.

The idea of a less hateful political culture isn't a fantasy, because we've enjoyed it before. Our last great consensus leader, Bob Hawke, was not elected with a mandate to open up the Australian economy. But he was able to do so because he first brought the country together. Then, like now, what mattered most was finding an economic direction for the country that was broadly shared – by many, if not by all. Of course, politics had conflict back then. But today governments seek out policies specifically because they know they will be opposed. Past governments – better governments – strove for the middle ground.

The role of government in a transitioning economy is to do what evidence shows us works. If we took that approach, we'd find the answers – and consensus about them – much more quickly than we are doing at the moment. In time, those interventions may come to be described as a coherent ideology. The neat way of describing the Hawke–Keating modernisation project didn't emerge until it was underway. In the meantime, we politicians have plenty to get on with – even if we don't yet know exactly how to define what we're doing.

Clare O'Neil

BALANCING ACT | Correspondence

Andrew Charlton and Jim Chalmers

At the end of George Megalogenis's discourse on the woes of Australian politics, he encapsulates the equal mixture of ambition, anxiety and ambivalence in Australia's current mood: "The only thing weighing us down," he quips, "is the chip on our shoulder." It's a wonderful line and a lovely Australian piss-take on America's nation-defining axiom, "The only thing we have to fear is fear itself."

Franklin Roosevelt spoke those words to a shaken nation on his first day as president of the United States: 4 March 1933. In the preceding four years, the US economy had shrunk by one-third. More than 20 million Americans were unemployed and those who did have jobs struggled to survive on wages that were barely above starvation levels. Contemporary observers worried that "capitalism itself was at the point of dissolution." A friend of Roosevelt's warned him that if he succeeded he would be remembered as the greatest president, but if he failed, as the worst. "If I fail," he replied, "I shall be the last."

Today Australia, and much of the world, is mired in the long shadow of another economic malaise. The global financial crisis was not comparable to the Great Depression, and latter-day parallels should not be overdone. But allowing for differences in scale, there are similarities in the challenges of both eras.

Most obviously, the global economy is again in a protracted period of slow growth. What began in the United States has spread to Europe and is now dragging down emerging markets. Australia, which many hoped had escaped the crisis, may just have been waiting its turn.

Megalogenis surveys the landscape and concludes that our "version of capitalism ... is broken." This motivates his essay's first argument: that we need to chart a new course because our policy frameworks are no longer fit for purpose. He is right and proved so by nearly a decade of anaemic global growth.

Megalogenis's second argument is that the answers to our predicament lie outside the mainstream Australian reform discourse. Again, he's spot-on.

Australia's reform discourse is dominated by business councils, economic journalists and the commentariat of retired public servants who cut their teeth in the Hawke–Keating era of liberalisation, which remains their north star. Deregulation, privatisation, workplace flexibility and tax cuts are the four walls of their economic worldview. But as Hyman Minsky said, "Those who long for the lost reform era must recognise that 'economies evolve and so, too, must economic policy.'"

Megalogenis astutely observes that Keating's liberalisation agenda worked to solve the challenges of the 1980s but isn't fit for purpose anymore because the economy is so different now. New challenges – digital disruption, automation of jobs, financial stability, inequality – need new solutions.

Megalogenis believes the alternative to Keating's open globalism is to throw back further in time. He believes that what is needed is more akin to the "post-war reconstruction of Curtin, Chifley and Menzies." He would like to see more investment in "physical infrastructure, education and innovation" and more done to address inequality.

All these are sensible propositions, but we should be looking forward rather than back to find the new economic model we need. Hawke and Keating built a policy edifice to address the defining challenge of their time: globalisation. Now another generation needs to build a response to a new challenge: the digitisation of the economy.

We need a policy framework that grapples with 21st-century economic challenges, such as:

1. How do we maintain hard-won workplace protections in an economy increasingly dominated by freelancers? (How do you make sure Uber drivers have sick leave?)
2. Is it okay for some companies to own huge amounts of personal consumption, health, financial and even genetic information? (Should personal data be private or perhaps a public good for the benefit of all?)
3. What is the role for small peripheral economies like Australia when so much economic activity is becoming dominated by global networked digital oligopolies? (Netflix, for example, had, until recently, nearly a million Australian customers, but almost no local employees.)
4. How do we go about taxing multinational companies in a digital economy where there is no "local production" and transfer pricing can approach 100 per cent?
5. How can we use digital technologies to reconceive public services? (Are huge productivity gains in health and education potentially within reach?)

Technological progress has made citizens more informed and globally connected than ever before. This has implications for economic policy and the role of government. We have to "rethink the state" once again in the context of a digital economy.

When FDR assumed the presidency, the US was crying out for a new direction that had been denied them under his predecessor, President Herbert Hoover, whose free-market ideology taught him to eschew government intervention to help the poor and revive the economy. Hoover's intransigence made him a figure of derision. The shantytowns of unemployed in the cities became known as "Hoovervilles" and the newspapers their residents used to stave off the cold were known as "Hoover blankets."

Roosevelt immediately promised "action, and action now." He shut the nation's banks the day after his inauguration. During the next hundred days, he delivered what historian Arthur Schlesinger Jr called "a presidential barrage of ideas and programs unlike anything known to American history." He attracted a new generation of reformers to Washington ("men with long hair and women with short hair," according to contemporary wags).

Australia's political situation calls for a similar response to our present malaise. Rarely in our history have we been less confident of our collective purpose, our environmental wellbeing and our economic security. We have no idea what sort of world we will be leaving our children to inherit. We need fresh ideas because we can no longer delude ourselves that the answers to new problems lie in the past.

Andrew Charlton and Jim Chalmers

BALANCING ACT | Correspondence

Tom Bentley and Jonathan West

"Will we have to wait for another crash before we find the model that restores stability to our twenty-first century?" In the last line of his Quarterly Essay, George Megalogenis asks exactly the right question for the situation Australia now faces. Our economy is out of kilter with global conditions and public expectations. Since the financial crisis of 2008, our political system has been spinning its wheels trying to gain traction on the big challenges – how to maintain prosperity, meet the needs of a changing, growing population and respond to destabilising global risks.

The central proposition of *Balancing Act* – that Australia should debate "a permanent change in the relationship between the state and the market" – is right. But to succeed, that debate needs to question the deeper assumptions and relationships underpinning the dominant policy consensus. Only then will we unlock the ideas that can shape another generation of inclusive growth. In *Time for a New Consensus*, an essay published concurrently with *Balancing Act*, we argue that Australia's policy elites are trapped within the narrow bounds of a consensus that has outlived its usefulness. That consensus, described in *Balancing Act* as the "open model," was constructed in the 1980s through collaborative, experimental leadership and dialogue across politics, the public service, the media, business and civil society. It was driven by the need to ensure all citizens would benefit from economic modernisation, when global stagnation forced a reconsideration of Australia's "federation" model, which itself had prevailed through most of the twentieth century.

The 1980s consensus fused neoliberal economic reforms with social insurance – Medicare, superannuation, HECS and now the National Disability Insurance Scheme. It underpinned economic growth for a quarter of a century and became globally influential. But its most productive and fruitful reforms were enacted twenty years ago. Now, the rising financial and political cost of extending economic deregulation and social insurance helps to explain the recent turbulence and rancour of federal politics. Since 2008, both sides of politics have struggled to reconcile conflicting expectations of economic growth, social investment and a balanced budget, amid increasingly shrill and antagonistic public debate. In a world where interest rates are at their lowest for five centuries, nation-states are going bankrupt, and climate change and inequality threaten global stability, the policy repertoire of the 1980s simply does not achieve traction.

Like any other nation, Australia cannot expect to maintain inclusive growth by default, or assume that a policy mix it helped to invent three decades ago will remain relevant or superior. So Megalogenis is right that a re-scoped economic policy agenda should include a much more active role for government in improving education and infrastructure, because the open model has not and cannot generate adequate solutions. He is also correct to point to low interest rates and public borrowing power as an opportunity to do this. But the issues he highlights – gridlocked cities, too-hot housing markets and growing educational inequality – are not the causes of our current situation, but symptoms of a deeper problem that must also be addressed.

In fact, the workings of the "open model" have transformed the structure of Australia's economy in ways that are now impeding adaptation and renewal. Amazingly, Australians emerged from a once-in-a-century resources boom more indebted than when we entered it. Bank lending increased between 1985 and 2015 from just above 20 per cent of GDP to almost 130 per cent. The main focus of this ballooning debt is housing. Australia has the world's highest ratio of housing debt to total lending (54 per cent compared to, for example, 16 per cent in the United States, 20 per cent in France, 40 per cent in the UK and 14 per cent in Hong Kong), and the world's second-highest ratio of mortgage debt to GDP (at 99 per cent, behind only Switzerland). As Megalogenis points out, housing is one of the *least* productive ways to invest. Lopsided lending for private housing has diverted finance away from business investment, which should be developing new products, services, infrastructure and jobs in non-mining sectors. Housing finance increased from less than 25 per cent of credit outstanding in 1990 to more than 60 per cent today; business lending declined from almost 65 per cent to less than 35 per cent over the same period. (Finance for new houses declined from 35 per cent of new commitments to 15 per cent today.) As a proportion of the economy, finance and real estate have soared from 7 per cent in 1975 to 12 per cent in 2015, while mining grew from 6 to 9 per cent, and manufacturing declined from almost 20 per cent to 7 per cent. Finance-sector profits increased from less than 1 per cent of GDP in 1985 to more than 5 per cent in 2015. The finance sector now makes up almost half (47.5 per cent) of the ASX200's total market value.

Australia's productive base beyond mining has actually narrowed or declined over this period. Minerals alone accounted for 59 per cent of merchandise exports in 2015. Rising wages and a high dollar have hollowed out domestic industry. For two decades, the impact has been masked by mining investment, rising house prices and escalating government expenditure.

In an economy that was adapting well to changing conditions, capital and knowledge would be invested in a wide range of activities and infrastructure, creating new products, services, technology applications and business processes. But this is not what the spectacular growth of private debt and financial transactions has been used for over the last generation.

In fact, the emphasis placed by the 1980s consensus on the importance of markets in allocating resources has helped to blind us to the risks of an economy over-concentrated in specific sectors and over-dependent on private debt and consumption. While market liberalisation created real gains, aided by an aggressive privatisation program, they were essentially one-offs. So too with free trade: despite the rapid growth of new markets in the Asia-Pacific region, the World Bank estimates that recently signed free-trade agreements will produce no GDP growth for Australia.

Deeper thought about the sources of productive growth is needed. As we discuss in detail in *Time for a New Consensus*, it is not markets that take decisions or invest resources – it is groups of people operating through institutions and networks. Global markets are a permanent feature of our landscape, but building the capabilities to thrive amid such competition is a matter of human effort – by businesses, communities, governments and civil society.

Building these dynamic capabilities should be the task of the next consensus. Focusing on comparative advantage – on those sectors capable of punching above their weight in global markets – will guide allocation of the nation's resources. It will also defend against the tendency within government towards administrative centralisation.

To do this successfully we must move beyond the static conception of the 1980s consensus, in which comparative advantage is assumed to arise simply from applying the discipline of market competition. This snapshot view fits neatly with a relentless emphasis on free trade and domestic competition. Not surprisingly, it ends up favouring those forms of advantage that are natural, geographically fixed and inherited – such as mineral resources. Over time, it ignores three crucial dimensions of economic development: differential industry growth, technological improvement and the divergent social impacts of different industries.

First, industries grow at very different rates as societies mature and develop. As nations emerge from poverty, demand for meat grows faster than for rice; it then tapers off once citizens can afford to eat their fill. Similarly, demand for automobiles at first grows faster than for bicycles, then tapers off, before (in the richest countries) reversing, as citizens place a premium on fitness. These differentials can create big problems for nations that specialise only in their field of natural comparative advantage. The East Asian nations that have improved so dramatically in recent decades have chosen to specialise in fast-growing manufacturing sectors, not slow-growing traditional parts of the economy.

Second, industries show very different technological potentials over time. England's textile producers spectacularly increased their output during the Industrial Revolution by introducing new machines and new techniques, driving productivity to unimagined heights; Portugal's winemakers, by contrast, were forced to continue growing grapes and pressing juice from them, with only marginal increases in output over time. This effect is even more marked today, with huge disparities in technology-driven productivity growth among industries, especially those close to the twin revolutions of information technology and biotechnology.

Third, and perhaps most importantly, different industries bring about divergent social consequences. Some generate more equality and greater opportunity for workers by relying far more on labour than machines or software. These usually drive higher skills and learning and allow wages to capture a much greater share output. In precision engineering and specialty chemicals, wages account for two-thirds output, and the operating surplus (from which equity holders draw their return) accounts for a mere 6 per cent. Others bifurcate into a small number of high-wage employees and a great amount of technology. In computers and life sciences, wages account for only 11 per cent and 7 per cent respectively of output.

These three characteristics make any policy effort to create comparative advantage a complex challenge. They demand a shift from one-off static advantage to cumulative, dynamic advantage, and they help to explain why the "open model" cannot cope with the transition to a post-mining-boom economy.

Market forces alone will not maintain both economic vitality and high social investment. And while governments should be more willing to use public borrowing and investment to counteract market failures, this is not enough. The new consensus must focus on how private enterprise and public policy can combine to create economic capability through investment, innovation and learning.

This will not be easy, but the three factors outlined above give an important clue about how it can be done. Comparative advantage in the twenty-first century demands *geographic and sectoral decentralisation*. Where past reformers sought to create seamless national and international markets, the next generation must focus on specialised sectors of the economy, which cluster differently from region to region.

This is a big shift, away from remote federal rule-making institutions and towards more dynamic, partnership-based efforts in city-regions. Because the old consensus sees the role of government as limited to neutral rule-maker and enforcer, diligently hunting down and eliminating sources of "rent-seeking," Australian political institutions and policy-makers have largely shed the ability to design and implement strategies at this level. But there are signs that the change is beginning, as state and city governments, universities and industry groups pursue a new agenda.

The 1980s consensus was not a set of timeless truths uncovered by Milton Friedman and Bob Hawke, but a specific set of propositions developed through persistent, collaborative effort. An equivalent process is needed today. It will not be easy, but Australia has succeeded before. *Balancing Act* is helping to open up the conversation we need to have.

Tom Bentley and Jonathan West

BALANCING ACT | Correspondence

Bob Katter

I was on the tally-room panel on Queensland election night when it was announced that Premier Campbell Newman had lost his seat and government. I observed that the implications were quite profound. The "average lifespan" of a premier in Queensland was now just 2.4 years, and this in a state where before 1990 there had been only one change of government in seventy-five years.

I then proceeded to provoke the panel by providing an explanation for this phenomenon. "In 1990, we, the Country Party, were running Queensland on a budget of just $8 billion – the ALP couldn't run it on $49 billion and the LNP needed $51 billion!"

A fellow panellist, the ex-Brisbane mayor Jim Soorley (ALP), pointedly commented, "Yeah, you and Leo Hielscher." (Leo was Under Treasurer of Queensland under Joh Bjelke-Petersen.)

I replied, "Well, more power to us." Soorley was undoubtedly right: Leo Hielscher and Sid Schubert delivered, as did the government, a very competent public service.

Laura Tingle's *Political Amnesia* shows the damage done by the politicisation of that "valuable repository of memory," the public service. Forthright advice and a sense of duty have been replaced by quiescence, or more properly a self-serving acquiescence. But Tingle's essay falls short of explaining why Queenslanders loved their governments so much for seventy-five years and yet dislike them so intensely now.

George Megalogenis's *Balancing Act* quite rightly asserts that "something deeper is happening here than the predictable incompetence of politics." Thoughtful people would agree. Not surprising, really, because people are now enduring the bitter harvest sewn by twenty-five years of market fundamentalism. What the Honourable Billy Wentworth called "marketisation" is the removal of all mechanisms of protection and support. This while the giants – the US, the EU and

Japan – have removed very little. I'll give but one example of this: world agriculture receives 41.5 per cent of its income from government, whereas Australian agriculture receives only 5.6 per cent. And while the giants have maintained their levels of support, the BRIC economies have remained aggressively interventionist.

Megalogenis avers that voters are asking for "a return to some form of government intervention in the economy" and that "this is resisted ... because of a misguided faith in the open economic model." It can be added that such faith is very bipartisan, deep-rooted and semi-religious. Consequent upon the mantras of "deregulation" and "National Competition Policy" becoming government fiat, the manufacture of motor vehicles in Australia has ceased, and gone is all whitegoods manufacture, as well as almost all manufacturing of footwear, clothing, personal accoutrements, watches, mobiles, biros and glasses.

Wool, up until deregulation, was Australia's biggest export commodity. Since deregulation, sheep numbers have declined by 64 per cent. Since deregulation, 31 per cent of the dairy herd has gone. Since deregulation, 17 per cent of our sugarcane production has gone. So too 20 per cent of the beef and veal cattle herd. Ironically, with cattle, this is a result of social interventionism: the ban on live cattle exports and the moratorium placed on all "on-farm" (micro) irrigation. And a propped up Australian dollar.

Not surprisingly, economic "anti"-interventionism has led to no Reconstruction Board and no ethanol. (The US and Brazil have ethanol, and as a consequence their cattle access the valuable byproduct distillers grain.)

The economic rationalists told us that "freeing the market" – getting rid of industries that need government "intervention" – will liberate resources to move into other industries. After twenty-five years we are entitled to ask, "What other industries?"

We're told, "service industries." Australians' future is to be waiting on tables and cleaning toilets for foreign visitors (tourism). Or are our universities to become visa shops (education)?

In the ten years before marketisation, electricity prices stayed almost static at a miniscule $740 per household. In the ten years following marketisation, prices shot up to $2347. Now we have the world's second-highest electricity charges. This prices us out of mineral processing. In April 2016 the steel plant in Whyalla and the nickel plant in North Queensland both announced they would close. Much of the NSW steel industry is also gone. Plans to expand aluminium at Gladstone have been scrapped.

Megalogenis's *Balancing Act* avers that the electorate is demanding intervention in the form of deficit budgeting. He is right, of course. The time-honoured aphorism says it well: "The people in pain will punish the people in power."

Megalogenis doesn't answer a question; he poses a question. He rightly points out that Kevin Rudd borrowed money for insulating your roof and improving school buildings. These generated more debt, but there was no increase in revenue to service this debt. The global financial crisis made this quick fix an imperative. History will undoubtedly applaud Rudd and Swan. But the point still holds: Labor offers social benefits and pork-barrelling, but this is more than offset by the growing burden of servicing the debt that results. This traditional approach is colourfully described by Professor John Quiggin as "Zombie Economics."

Professor Brian Galligan long ago delineated how the Queensland Country Party government borrowed nearly half a billion dollars for just two items. This was on an annual state budget of less than $1 billion – it was deficit budgeting on a cosmic scale.

Half of this money was spent building ports, coal loaders and rail lines for the (yet to be developed) Queensland coalfields. The other half was spent building the "world's biggest" power station. There were no contracted customers for the coal, nor for the electricity. This truly was government venture financing on a grand scale.

Until the 1960s most referred to Queensland as the State of Stagnation. The 1966 Queensland Year Book recorded coal production of a miniscule 1.6 million tonnes, while aluminium production was nil. By 1986 coal was 69 million tonnes per year. In today's money that is $5 billion a year. In 1986 Queensland produced 3 million tonnes of alumina and aluminium (in today's money, earnings of over $1 billion a year).

Macro-analysis removes Canberra from reality and communicates in a language that only esoteric commentators understand. Government and the Roman Church used Latin in the Middle Ages to prevent people from participating in matters of importance. The expert commentator speaking jargon can get away with not having the slightest clue what he is talking about.

Back in the land of reality, clearly the way forward is deficit budgeting – borrowing money – but only money to create development. What will we get for the $5-billion tunnel announced by the Newman (Qld LNP) government, or Bill Shorten's $5000-million River Rail crossing. To quote the *Courier-Mail*, in a wonderful piece of irony, "it will get you home 15 minutes earlier to watch the TV."

If this money goes not to self-indulgence but to development, it can build the

NT–Qld border canal, the rail-line into the Galilee coalfields, the dam projects south-west of Cairns and Townsville – new industries creating $15 billion a year into the indefinite future.

Let me be very specific: the current situation of buying everything from overseas but selling nothing to pay for it is the Path to Perdition.

The question remains: will we walk into the land of reality? Or continue on ever deeper into the ideological wilderness?

Bob Katter

BALANCING ACT | Correspondence

Saul Eslake

George Megalogenis writes about today's economy with a grasp of the broad sweep of Australian history and an awareness of the social consequences of economic performance and policy – attributes which have been all too rare among economic commentators of the past two decades. He is thus able to diagnose aspects of Australia's economic performance – and the strengths and weaknesses of Australian economic policy-making – which elude many others.

In *Balancing Act*, Megalogenis draws attention to what he sees as the shortcomings of Australian economic management during and after the China-driven "commodities boom," which, together with the global financial crisis of 2008–09 and its aftermath, has been the most important phenomenon shaping Australia's economic experience thus far in the twenty-first century.

There is much to admire in Megalogenis's analysis of this period. But his prognosis – that Australia has entered a "danger zone," where "a recession of some kind will be difficult to avoid" – does not follow ineluctably from that analysis. And his proposed course of treatment hardly amounts to the radical surgery that he suggests it does.

With the exception of China itself, probably no other country benefited as much from China's rapid economic growth, industrialisation and urbanisation as Australia. This was because Australia's resource endowment was uniquely suited to China's needs. Of the four commodities at the heart of China's transformation – iron ore, coal, oil and LNG – Australia, alone among the world's major commodity exporters, possessed three in ample quantities. Moreover, Australia also benefited from China's emergence as a major manufacturing exporter, so that we paid lower prices for imported manufactured goods.

Australia's terms of trade – the ratio of the prices received for our exports to the prices paid for our imports – improved by 97 per cent between 2000 and their peak in 2011. No other commodity-exporting nation gained as much: over the same interval, Canada's terms of trade improved by 18 per cent, New Zealand's by 26 per cent, Norway's and Brazil's by 39 and 40 per cent respectively, and South Africa's by 42 per cent. Only Russia and Chile came close to recording terms of trade gains close to Australia's, but even they fell around 10 percentage points short of our gains. And of course for most of Australia's peers among the advanced economies, this rise in the prices of commodities and fall in the prices of manufactures represented a loss of income, rather than a gain as it did for Australia.

Megalogenis is right to point out that during this period, Australia's (public) finances "suddenly assumed the character of a magic pudding." As the Parliamentary Budget Office has recently calculated, between 2002–03 and 2008–09 "parameter variations" (that is, unexpected windfalls) boosted revenues by a minimum of $222 billion. Yet, rather than save the bulk of this in a form of "sovereign wealth fund" – as Ross Garnaut, Chris Richardson and I advocated at the time – to be drawn down in order to cushion the inevitable downturn after commodity prices peaked at some (then unknowable) point in the future – the Howard government (in its last five years in office) and the Rudd government (in its first year) spent the lot, and more – giving away, according to the PBO's calculations, $89 billion in tax cuts and deliberately increasing spending by $175 billion.

This was when the "age of entitlement" which Joe Hockey bemoaned in 2012 was created. And it was then that the seeds of Australia's present budgetary difficulties were sown – although they were subsequently well watered by the Gillard government's inability to reverse the spending increases undertaken during the financial crisis, and its insistence on yet more discretionary increases in entitlement spending. As Megalogenis concludes, "we ... failed to live up to our own previous high standard of prudence."

Precisely because Australia benefited so much from the "up" phase of the commodities boom, it was almost inevitable that we would find the subsequent "down" phase difficult – especially since we did so little to prepare for it. Since 2011 Australia's terms of trade have deteriorated by 29 per cent. Apart from Russia, whose terms of trade have fallen by 30 per cent over this period, no other commodity-exporting nation has seen a similar decline: Brazil's have fallen by 18 per cent, Norway's by 14 per cent, Chile's by 12 per cent, Canada's by 10 per cent, and South Africa's by 9 per cent, while New Zealand's terms of trade have actually risen by 3 per cent over this period (though they have declined from a somewhat later peak in 2014). And of course most other advanced economies' terms of trade have improved since 2011.

The remarkable thing, therefore, is not that Australia's economic performance has deteriorated since the peak in commodity prices in 2011 – which, of course, it has – but rather that Australia has thus far managed this challenging period better than virtually all of the other countries which gained much less than us from the "up" phase of the commodities boom, and thus *prima facie* had less to fear during the "down" phase.

Australia has *not* experienced a recession, in the widely used sense of that term, as Canada and (more dramatically) Brazil and Russia have. Australia's growth rate has slowed, to be sure – to 2.5 per cent in 2015 – but not as much as Chile's (2.1 per cent), Norway's (1.7 per cent) or South Africa's (1.3 per cent). Our unemployment rate is higher than at the peak of the boom, but it has risen by less than in South Africa, Brazil and Norway, and remains lower than in Canada. Of the commodity-exporters with which it is legitimate to compare Australia, only New Zealand has weathered the "down" phase of the boom better than Australia – and, as noted earlier, the "down" phase for New Zealand has been both more recent and milder than for hard-commodity exporters like Australia.

Far from demonstrating the limitations of Australia's "open model," as Megalogenis calls it, Australia's comparative resilience is, arguably, a vindication of it. An open door to (authorised) migration (giving Australia a faster rate of population growth than most other commodity-exporting, or "advanced," economies), a capacity and willingness to cut interest rates to record lows, a flexible exchange rate, a more flexible labour market than most conservative critics are prepared to acknowledge, and a willingness to eschew the more dramatic forms of fiscal austerity pursued in most other advanced economies – all these things together have served Australia very well.

Megalogenis's more telling observation is that we *could* have done even better – had, as he cogently and persuasively argues, Australian governments (federal and state) been willing to spend significantly more on infrastructure. Not only would our economy have been stronger, but so would the quality of life in our cities – and maybe in some of our regions – have improved too.

Australia would have been better placed to spend more on much-needed infrastructure if we hadn't frittered away so many – indeed, more than all – of the gains that accrued to governments during the "up" phase of the boom. As the Reserve Bank Governor, Glenn Stevens, has pointed out, albeit subtly, on several occasions, we could have done this had governments been more willing to borrow at the record-low long-term interest rates available to them in recent years. The appetite for Australian government debt suggests that both local and foreign investors would have financed infrastructure spending equivalent to at least one, and possibly more than two, percentage points of GDP – provided that the infrastructure projects were demonstrably well chosen, and especially if successive (federal) governments had sought to improve their "operating" budget positions over this period.

But even if, as Megalogenis advocates, infrastructure spending "should probably return to the levels of the 1960s, when it was closer to 10 per cent of GDP," this hardly amounts to a repudiation of the "open model," where "four key prices – the currency, interest rates, tariffs and wages" are "removed … from political control." On the contrary – as Megalogenis acknowledges at one point – it represents an "augmentation" of that model. We now have what Megalogenis calls for – "a Reserve Bank–style model … to identify and rank projects on economic and social grounds, and to recommend timelines for implementation" – in the form of Infrastructure Australia. We simply need to provide stronger guarantees of its independence from governments, and more powerful incentives for them to follow its recommendations.

Much the same is true of Megalogenis's other suggestions. He's right to draw attention to the risks associated with Australia's love affair with property investment, and the role that Australia's tax system has played in promoting that form of infatuation. And, yes, it would have been better if negative gearing had been curtailed during the global financial crisis – a suggestion which Wayne Swan repudiated upon belatedly releasing the Henry Review in May 2010, even though the Henry Review hadn't actually recommended it – or, indeed, at any time in the past three decades. But that's no reason to cavil at doing so now. Indeed, as Megalogenis says elsewhere, "the political dialogue about tax has to change": but with the exception of superannuation, he doesn't say where, or how.

Similarly, he's right to draw attention to Australia's below-average rate of female workforce participation, especially compared to Canada or New Zealand. However, Megalogenis's recommendation amounts to a plea for prime ministers to follow Canadian prime minister Justin Trudeau's example in allocating Cabinet positions among men and women – sound advice, to be sure, but hardly a radical expansion of the role of government in the economy.

Megalogenis's essay doesn't really amount to an argument for much bigger government – such as Jeff Madrick, who at one time held a similar role at the *New York Times* to the one Megalogenis held at the *Australian*, sought to make in the aptly titled *The Case for Big Government* (2009). Rather, it is a plea for better government – government which looks, thinks and plans ahead, which does what governments are supposed to do and does it well, which is willing and able to "lean against" the "irrational exuberance" to which markets are from time to time inclined, and which is concerned about issues like fairness and opportunity. As such, it's both well-argued and timely.

Saul Eslake

BALANCING ACT | *Correspondence*

Paul Strangio

George Megalogenis's thought-provoking Quarterly Essay resonates with the widely held view that 21st-century Australia is mired in policy inertia, with successive federal governments having had neither the imagination nor the foresight to devise a coherent plan for the economy or society.

While Megalogenis is advocating for an invigorated state, he wisely indicates that this is an undertaking not solely for those situated at the apex of executive government. As with previous eras of major transformation (the 1940s and 1980s), this project needs to be "collaborative." On those earlier occasions, "strong bonds of trust existed between politics, bureaucracy, and the press, between the representatives of labour, capital and welfare." This may be a somewhat rose-tinted view of the politics of those times, but the fundamental point stands. Meaningful and enduring reform is more likely to spring from distributed leadership and a community of ideas rather than the centralised decision-making favoured by recent prime ministers. As such, it is a little incongruous that the essay ultimately places so much weight on whether Malcolm Turnbull is the leader who can propel Australia towards the desired reconstruction ("He has to author a new model *and* run a long-term government").

Megalogenis notes that for Turnbull and the Liberals, embracing an activist state means defying their natural philosophical instincts – an inversion of Labor's support for market economics in the 1980s. On the other hand, though Megalogenis doesn't draw this connection, the logic of his analysis is that the policy cycle is gravitating in a direction more compatible with Labor traditions. He does observe that of recent prime ministers, the only one "who seriously tried to find a way out of the [policy] impasse was Rudd, but he lost focus after the global financial crisis." My view is that it was under Julia Gillard's leadership that Labor showed the most resolve in pursuing a persuasive post-market program. The ingredients included a carbon tax (accelerating the transition to a post-carbon economy will surely be integral to any significant future reform project); a needs-based education funding model; the National Disability Insurance Scheme (renewing the social contract); and the National Broadband Network. The politics, however, were hopelessly loaded against Gillard and she showed a frustrating incapacity to articulate how the aforementioned elements constituted a cohesive agenda.

To my mind, one of the most interesting aspects of *Balancing Act* is the way in which Megalogenis uses history as a reference point and is alive to past policy cycles. He suggests that what Australia needs is a paradigm shift equivalent to two previous policy turning points: the post-war reconstruction of the 1940s, and the 1980s market liberalisation. It is a point worth developing. There is some intriguing North American political science literature that analyses the rise and fall of policy regimes and examines how they correlate with, and help determine, the cycles of (presidential) politics. We can discern something roughly similar when we reflect upon the patterns of twentieth-century Australia. The interwar period has long been recognised as one marked by political stasis and policy stagnation. A new order had to await the election of the Curtin government, its senior members steeled, as Megalogenis observes, by the abject experience of Jim Scullin's Depression-era Labor administration. They also harnessed new (Keynesian-inspired) ideas and strengthened institutional arrangements through the recruitment of "experts" to the heart of government and by collaborating with an invigorated public service to usher in the managed economy. In turn, that model was consolidated during the long boom presided over by Robert Menzies.

By the late 1960s, however, the post-war policy settlement came under strain as international financial arrangements fractured and domestic economic disorder grew. Australian politics entered another period of instability and policy flux, with governments either clinging to established verities or pre-emptively seeking a fresh direction at a point when conditions were not yet fully ripe. It was, of course, the Hawke–Keating Labor government, learning from the chaos of the Whitlam years, but also benefiting from the gestation of deregulatory ideas and the maturing of institutional innovations begun under its Labor predecessor, that instigated a new market-based policy settlement in the 1980s. This was entrenched in the early years of John Howard's prime ministership. Since the early 2000s, however, there have been signs of regime decay, manifested in a return to policy complacency (Megalogenis is biting about the negligence of Howard's latter terms), the proliferation of intractable problems and an outbreak of political skittishness, set against the background of increased global uncertainty.

Needless to say, the notion of large-scale policy cycles cannot by itself account for recent political upheavals and policy confusion (the altered media landscape, party decline and institutional disequilibrium are clearly contributing), but nor is it irrelevant. Policy cycles can indeed help us understand why opportunities for governments and their leaders wax and wane over time: they are not all created equal. In any case, we should be grateful to George Megalogenis for challenging us to look beyond the existing (declining) status quo and for his brave intuition of the coming policy wave.

Paul Strangio

BALANCING ACT | Correspondence

Elizabeth Humphrys and Tad Tietze

Like Paul Kelly, George Megalogenis is one of those rare journalists who integrates economic, social and cultural developments into his political narrative and policy proposals. His writing is among the most insightful and empirically substantiated of its kind, superior to both the efforts of fellow journalists and much of the recent academic literature on Australian politics. He gets beyond personality-based non-explanations of political success and failure to arrive at deeper structural causes.

But one issue undermines the agenda he spells out in *Balancing Act*. Do politicians and governments any longer have the capacity to carry through a serious socio-economic reform program *of any kind*?

Megalogenis contrasts today's political malaise with the Curtin and Hawke reform periods:

> On the previous two occasions when Australia reinvented itself, in the 1940s and 1980s, it was taken for granted that the project would be collaborative. Strong bonds of trust existed between politics, bureaucracy and the press, and between the representatives of labour, capital and welfare. Those connections have been broken by a culture that favours the attention-seeker over the expert, and the bully over the consensus-builder.

In doing so he provides an explanation of reform success that relies on somewhat ill-defined cultural concepts – "bonds of trust," "expertise" and "consensus-building" – without asking what material foundations these were built on and whether they still exist. Indeed, those two previous "reinventions" were marked by something that has been missing in recent decades: the organised social bases of the political system, and in particular labourism's mass trade union base.

The relationship between a powerful but conservative trade union bureaucracy and the ALP was the fulcrum of Australian politics from the early years of the twentieth century. In simple terms, the unions formed the ALP to have representation in the political sphere, and conservative parties united in opposition to that. It is no coincidence that serious reform was often the work of Labor governments: their close connection to unions of key industries meant that organised workers could at times play a consensual role in economic change, even though at other times they locked horns with employers and governments. The conservative side of politics, allied to business interests, tended to operate more as an antagonist to labour's power than an agenda-setting force of its own.

But the effect of the 1980s reforms was to hollow out the ALP–union link and, more importantly, to *disorganise* the working-class base of the unions. These changes have greatly undermined the ability of politicians to implement far-reaching national economic reforms – simply because they no longer have institutional partners with a serious social base in civil society with whom to develop trust, mobilise expertise and build consensus.

Crucially, Hawke and Keating's key macro-economic policy tool was a corporatist contract between unions and government (with only informal business support). The Accord – initially laced with the promise of price controls to restrain runaway inflation, industry restructuring in the interests of job creation and dramatic increases in social spending – rapidly became little more than a blunt instrument for the infliction of centralised real wage cuts. With the enthusiastic participation in the Accord of (previously) militant unions like the AMWU, workers were persuaded to accept large sacrifices "in the national interest" in what was almost certainly the biggest consciously implemented upward redistribution of wealth in Australian history. Organised labour – and its ability to increase its exploitation by accepting "wage restraint" on a national basis – was offered up as the critical tool of macro-economic policy.

One obvious consequence was a fall in rates of unionisation, which declined from over 50 per cent in 1983 to just 31 per cent after Keating lost office in 1996, and continued to fall to a derisory 15 per cent in 2014. While this fall is not solely attributable to the Accord, the widespread suppression of wages and industrial action saw the ALP and ACTU disorganise their own base. The centralised nature of the unions' compact with the government required that the ACTU and union leaders quell workplace disputes, police those unions that threatened the deal's stability, and shift the locus of union activity from workplace organisation to high-level negotiations with government and legal argument in the Industrial Relations Commission (IRC). At ground level the effect was devastating: rapid erosion of rank-and-file participation in union activity, and a consequent weakening of the social weight and power of unions themselves. Archived minutes from local AMWU groups disclose a tragic tale of proud members watching in pain as the union they had built up systematically wound down its basic rank-and-file structures.

The unions tried to cover over this loss of power, first with a series of mergers and then with a campaign to replace centralised wage fixing with enterprise bargaining. Megalogenis assigns responsibility for enterprise bargaining to Keating, but the unions were the ones to demand it – desperate for a way to recover the drastic wage cuts of the 1980s. The new bargaining system was initially opposed by the IRC and key employers because of fear of revived militancy, but they needn't have worried: by the early 1990s unions were so weak that they were forced to accept a legal framework that effectively confined better organised workers' gains to single workplaces (with a paltry safety net for weaker groups of workers). Wages rose again in the Howard years, driven not by industrial militancy or government policy but by labour shortages in a booming economy, and they have stalled now that the economy has slowed.

Accompanying this, the social bases of both sides of politics, employer peak bodies and the non-government sector also faded. The leaderships of these organisations have become increasingly isolated and detached from their constituencies, just as civic participation in politics has withered on the vine. Labor Party angst that working-class voters can no longer be relied upon is paralleled by Liberal Party exasperation that employers don't go into bat for it when it pushes aggressively pro-business policies.

All this helps explain why periodic calls for new national-level cooperation among governments, employers, unions and other interest groups never get very far. This is not a matter of absent political will, or some "cultural" failure of the system. Rather, no section of the political class can claim to be practically tied to an organised bloc of civil society – certainly not one as economically crucial as organised labour – and so have the clout to make an impact on the political economy on a national scale. Further, it is not just that governments have allowed markets too much power in economic life, but that the changes of the last thirty-five years have left governments with ever-fewer levers with which to subvert blind market logic. Instead, we see at most a nebulous hope that infrastructure spending (that is, a sophisticated form of the state throwing money at economic processes beyond its control) can address the problems we face as a society.

We believe that no matter how brilliant and balanced a reform program is concocted by the best minds in the country, the coming years will be characterised by the persistence of a mostly reactive approach by governments to economic developments, and the inability of any section of the political class to develop an agenda that might consistently carry a majority of voters, let alone reshape society in line with this. The deeper structural factors we have outlined mean that pragmatic twists and turns, incoherent policy-making and political chaos are not about to exit the national stage.

Elizabeth Humphrys and Tad Tietze

BALANCING ACT | Correspondence

Henry Sherrell

Underlying much of George Megalogenis's excellent Quarterly Essay is the subject of immigration and population. Most people are acutely aware that Australia has a growing population. As Megalogenis explains, we are experiencing increasing congestion, and his section on housing reaffirms that something is askew: supply has failed to keep up with demand. Nation-building, with foundations of social cohesion and economic prosperity, remains a work in progress when the papers can thunder about how "foreigners" buy all the houses at Saturday auctions (note: Australians can have brown skin).

But fewer people understand that a massive shift in immigration policy since the mid-1990s has been the dominant factor behind population growth. As the rate of births and deaths is relatively stable, changes in Australia's population trends are driven by migration. Megalogenis doesn't explicitly say why our population growth kicked up a notch over the past two decades while the populations of many other rich countries stagnated. This is understandable – given the need for brevity – yet unfortunate, as he is one of a handful of people who could explain this neatly.

Nearly every informed commentator could write a volume on how the deregulation of trade and financial policy since the 1980s has fundamentally changed Australia. Yet the effect of immigration on our labour markets and urban centres remains poorly understood, despite having a deep impact on the day-to-day lives of millions of people.

The key shift is government control. From the post-war era of mass migration until about the early 1990s, the federal government controlled how many people came to Australia. Every year, a number was chosen, broadly based on the economic cycle. Low unemployment meant more migrants, while in times of recession it was made more difficult to migrate to Australia. Today, governments can only manage the flow of people to and from Australia. They cannot control the total number of migrants, because of two policy changes: the introduction of temporary migration, and the new priority given to economic over social and familial considerations.

Three of the largest groups of new migrants – international students, temporary skilled workers (457 visa holders) and backpackers (under the working holiday program) – are each "temporary," at least in name. Importantly, the government of the day does not determine the size of each of these categories. Instead, a combination of factors – such as labour demand, the exchange rate and universities, among others – affects migration to and from Australia. These uncapped classes of visas rise and fall from year to year.

Governments have been somewhat disingenuous about this. Tight border protection is trumpeted, yet it affects only a tiny minority of those seeking to come to Australia. Consultation between government and the electorate is moot, as the government only sets the number of permanent resident visas granted each year. Decades of growth, coupled with non-government bodies driving immigration policy, have led to a "new normal." Employers sponsor overseas workers, universities accept growing numbers of international students, and backpackers are pushed and pulled by the relative economic forces of different countries. Government has stepped back and today oversees this process at arm's length.

While some people are aware of this new normal, far too few consider the effect of immigration on employment, housing, infrastructure, urban policy and innovation. Even the Treasury, with its oft-repeated focus on the "three Ps" (population, participation and productivity) in such documents as the Intergenerational Reports, has largely failed to acknowledge how important immigration has been over the past fifteen years.

Why does this lack of understanding matter?

Right now, countries we share an affinity with, the United States and the United Kingdom, show what can occur if we ignore deep-rooted economic concerns and allow immigrants to become scapegoats. Donald Trump's proposed wall on the Mexican border and his rejection of Muslims are illustrations of this. It's not that his supporters are stupid, it's that they want a decent job and to feel safe. A wonky academic paper showing Mexican immigration has no negative effects on the average high-school drop-out cannot compete with the emotional battering experienced by those who have been left behind by the modern economy.

In a similar, but distinctly British, manner, the United Kingdom has contemplated leaving the European Union predominantly because migrant-baiting has become a quasi-national sport. Migration is the key issue driving the UK away from one of the most successful geopolitical projects in the history of the West.

Forget Margaret Thatcher, it was the cheap Romanian brickie that did it, or so goes the argument.

We have yet to experience this ugly face of anti-migration, anti-globalisation politics fully in Australia. We should not be held hostage to these positions, given that migration has a largely benign impact on our economy if appropriate responses are taken with regard to infrastructure, public services and crowded cities. At the margins, migration to Australia also reduces inequality and builds real links with our region.

To date, our political system has removed the possibility of a pedestal or megaphone. The Reclaim Australia movement lacks strong foundations, and formal parties like Australia First fail to penetrate the mainstream. Yet they linger on the edges of our society. Those who have been left behind, shut out and not given a hand-up will be the first to flock to such groups when the economy stops growing, as people give up on aspiration and opportunity.

Informed discussion and considered responses from government about our population and immigration policies, combined with continued prosperity, are the only serious bulwarks against this discourse infecting Australian politics. Here, Megalogenis is right on the mark. Government intervention – harnessing the immigration system that has emerged and responding to the structural change it has caused – is the best tool Australia has to remain a cohesive society that takes pride in its diversity.

Henry Sherrell

BALANCING ACT | *Correspondence*

Verity Firth

On 22 June 1944 President Franklin D. Roosevelt signed the *Servicemen's Readjustment Act* into law. The G.I. Bill, as it became known, was the greatest infrastructure investment in America's history. It provided returning veterans with tuition and living expenses to attend university, secondary school or vocational education. It also provided them with low-income mortgages and low-interest loans to start a business. As Stewart Brand concludes in *The Clock of the Long Now*, "The GI Bill's cost of $14.5 billion was paid back eightfold in taxes in the next twenty years, it jump-started the boom years of the 1950s, it built the world's largest middle class, and it set the nation decades ahead as the world moved into a knowledge economy."

The horrors of World War II created a sense of generational responsibility in governments and citizens alike that not only led to an economic boom, helped along by public investment in education and infrastructure, but also caused the only recorded period in human history where economic inequality was noticeably reduced.

We live in very different times. The victory of neoliberalism has allowed for an all-consuming belief that economies are best left to run by themselves. We have witnessed a hollowing out of public investment and a subsequent and related decline in public trust in government and institutions.

George Megalogenis makes a good case for intervention – he writes about Sydney, and more recently Melbourne, choking from the lack of public transport infrastructure; he offers a powerful comparison of percentages of GDP spent on public infrastructure compared with private investment in the residential property market; and he denounces the increasingly self-interested role of business in Australia in urging short-term goals against the longer-term good of the nation.

Megalogenis outlines the impact of the Rudd–Gillard government's stimulus package, delivered during the global financial crisis, and in particular the success of the Building the Education Revolution (BER) program. Despite the BER's obviously positive effect on the economy, Megalogenis notes with dismay that "Labor could not make that case to the electorate." Megalogenis links this failure to "sell" the BER to the decline in confidence among the political class that they should be interfering in the economy at all. Even with the obvious successes of the GFC stimulus package, he says, the Rudd–Gillard government couldn't wait to get out of there. Today's politicians have convinced themselves that a nation's budget is "out of their hands," that only two years' intervention was needed before the budget could revert to "neutral gear, neither slowing nor speeding up the economy" and the market could be allowed to return to doing what it does so well: running the economy. Megalogenis writes: "Governments forgot that markets and central banks can fail just as spectacularly as interventionist politicians."

While I agree with Megalogenis about the existence of a general ideological reticence to intervene, it is important to remember the circumstances surrounding the stimulus package and the reasons the Labor government had trouble "selling" it. The essence of any stimulus package is speed. You need to deliver the stimulus quickly and to the right sectors of the economy so as to maintain confidence and activity over time. As the economist Joseph Stiglitz noted, in many other countries the stimulus was too small and arrived too late, after jobs and confidence had already been lost. Premiums are to be expected in programs that are rolled out rapidly. In the BER program in New South Wales, managing contractors had hard deadlines for commencement of building works and for the completion of those works; the NSW Auditor-General later costed this premium at around 5 per cent on top of business as usual. However, media responses were rarely balanced enough to compare the costs of the package with its objects or outcomes, which included the maintenance of the building and trades sector and the safeguarding of 200,000 jobs Australia-wide. One newspaper mounted a daily crusade against the very concept of a stimulus package, and the BER in particular. This, combined with an extremely partisan (and effective) Opposition, created a hostile environment for a government pursuing a bold economic intervention.

Despite being the envy of the rest of the world, the Labor government suffered political fallout in the pursuit of economic stimulus. Opponents were well resourced and well coordinated. The "debt and deficit" narrative, however misplaced in the context of the GFC, haunts Labor to this day.

The lack of an evidence-based approach to the role of government investment in the economy is profoundly depressing, as is the fact that the Australian media are so willing to become political players and arbitrators of the public good while adopting the short game of analysis rather than the long view.

However, there is no time for recriminations. Megalogenis highlights research by Professor Bob Gregory that shows that migrants account for virtually all the full-time jobs created in Australia since 2007. "They didn't displace the local-born; they just took the cream of what was on offer, most notably in the professions." To avoid the political upheavals occurring in Trump's America or the UKIP's Britain, Australian governments must invest to ensure local-born young people have the skills needed to succeed in today's knowledge economy and obtain the high-end jobs the new economy provides. In Sydney and Melbourne, where housing prices and government policies are pushing working-class residents from the inner city out to cheaper housing on the urban fringe, we see access to these new-economy jobs becoming increasingly remote for the local-born.

Investing in education at this time makes sense. For the individual, the benefits are substantial in terms of employability and income; for the government, early investment in education reduces the longer-term costs of social services and welfare; and for the nation, such investment will allow us to adapt as the minerals boom subsides and ensure that Australians are equally equipped to seize the opportunities of the new global economy. And yet, at the time of writing, the federal government still won't commit to the additional years of the Gonski funding, and it still plans to proceed with significant cuts to the higher education budget. Hoisted on its own petard regarding "debt and deficit," it is striving to be seen to be reining in the budget and making promised cuts.

So how do you break this impasse? How do you give governments the courage to pursue bold initiatives? How do you re-create Megalogenis's "strong bonds of trust [that] existed between politics, bureaucracy and the press, and between the representatives of labour, capital and welfare" on the other occasions when Australia reinvented itself – in the 1940s and 1980s? Surely economic crisis and major war are not the only mechanisms to precipitate such policy intervention? If that is the case, we will be on course to fulfil the second of Megalogenis's predictions: "We will either catch the next wave of prosperity, or finally succumb to the great recession."

Verity Firth

BALANCING ACT | Response to Correspondence

George Megalogenis

One of the delightful challenges of a politics-heavy Quarterly Essay is the shelf-life of the subject matter. The risk is that a prime minister or opposition leader will implode on deadline, or soon after publication, dating the essay before the quarter is up. Malcolm Turnbull was the foundation victim of the QE curse, and its most recent beneficiary. Annabel Crabb's profile of the then Opposition leader, *Stop At Nothing* (Quarterly Essay 34), was released at the end of June 2009, a matter of days after Turnbull was forced to make a humiliating apology to Kevin Rudd, whom he had falsely accused of corruption based on the fabricated evidence of a rogue Treasury officer. Twenty-five essays later, in September 2015, Turnbull reversed the hex by toppling Tony Abbott as David Marr was finalising his profile of Bill Shorten, *Faction Man* (Quarterly Essay 59).

As I completed *Balancing Act*, I wondered if the curse would assume a new form, mocking my earnest attempt to start a debate about our economic model. A festival of innovation from Turnbull and his reinvigorated government could easily have made my modest proposals to renew our system appear dull on arrival. No such luck. With every idea he floated and discarded – a cut to the corporate tax rate, allowing the states to levy their own income taxes – Turnbull demonstrated that he had learnt nothing from the mistakes of the Rudd–Gillard–Abbott era. He didn't explain the problem he wanted to solve, or allow time for options to be discussed before the policy was finalised. I thought he would be smarter than that.

Paul Strangio points to an apparent contradiction in my argument. He agrees that genuine change requires collaboration. "Meaningful and enduring reform," he writes, "is more likely to spring from distributed leadership and a community of ideas rather than the centralised decision-making favoured by recent prime ministers. As such, it is a little incongruous that the essay ultimately places so much weight on whether Malcolm Turnbull is the leader who can propel Australia towards the desired [policy] reconstruction."

I was setting the challenge, not making a prediction. The public had projected onto Turnbull the role of saviour, and so the question for me was how that might work. Restoring a sense of shared purpose to the system begins with a conscious act of leadership to let go of the excessive but counterproductive power that has accumulated in the prime minister's office over the past twenty years. Greater freedom for the commonwealth public service, and cooperation with Labor and conservative states, are crucial elements of any project for more active government. Turnbull had ticked the first box, but not the second. He was the first national leader since Paul Keating to champion the bureaucracy. By contrast, his initial handling of the premiers was more Abbott-like than I expected. I know his polling told him that the public was frustrated with service delivery at the state level, and in any disagreement between jurisdictions voters would err on the side of the commonwealth. But the fight he picked at the Council of Australian Governments meeting in April was juvenile. He left the meeting without a tax policy, and with the threat of more intransigence to come on funding for public schools.

At the time of writing, the federal budget and the prime minister's trip to Government House to start the formal election campaign were only a matter of days away. The safe thing to do, then, is step over the landmines of the present and imagine what a new economic and political model might look like, based on the feedback from the correspondents.

Andrew Charlton and Jim Chalmers provide a neat summary of the challenge. For Hawke and Keating in the 1980s, it was globalisation. For this generation, it is "the digitisation of the economy." Technology is accelerating the shift in power from labour to capital in the domestic economy, and the shift from local business to globally networked oligopolies. While governments will find it difficult to collect tax from companies operating across borders, technology also provides the opportunity to revolutionise public services. "Are huge productivity gains in health and education potentially within reach?" Charlton and Chalmers ask. I hope so.

Clare O'Neil sees government involvement in the economy in the twenty-first century as a practical, rather than an ideological, issue. "We may not be looking at a new economic orthodoxy, but rather a shift away from orthodoxy altogether." The "guiding principle," she says, should be for intervention where the evidence shows that governments "can make a difference."

Tom Bentley and Jonathan West take the idea of intervention much further than other correspondents. They want to move "away from remote federal rulemaking institutions and towards more dynamic, partnership-based efforts in city-regions." Their vision for a model in which state governments and local councils wield more power raises two very obvious questions for me: can a fragmented system collect enough tax, and how will it avoid the trap of increasing inequality between cities and regions? While Victorians, for instance, might cheer a state government that can restore funding for the arts that was cut by a vindictive federal government, a bush council in Queensland will not have the means to maintain a critical mass of working-age people to provide for a population that is much older than the national average.

Among the correspondents, the optimists comfortably outnumber the pessimists. But I share the concern of Elizabeth Humphrys and Tad Tietze about the ability of the political system to mobilise community support for a new model. The two previous examples of national reinvention in the 1940s and 1980s relied, in part, on the Labor Party's links with the trade unions. As Humphrys and Tietze explain, the mass and active membership base meant "organised workers could at times play a consensual role in economic change, even though at other times they locked horns with employers and governments." As recently as 1983, half the workforce belonged to trade unions; now the figure is just 15 per cent.

The reasons for the collapse in coverage are complex, and they mirror the hollowing out of the main political parties themselves. But it does not necessarily follow that a new model is unobtainable in a world where large numbers of people no longer join political parties or trade unions, or go to church. Unlike earlier projects, the idea of an active government already has widespread public support.

I am grateful to everyone who replied to my essay and look forward to continuing this conversation.

George Megalogenis

Tom Bentley is a writer and policy adviser. He was the director of Demos, a London-based think-tank, and deputy chief of staff to Prime Minister Julia Gillard. He is the co-author, with Jonathan West, of the Griffith REVIEW ebook *Time for a New Consensus*.

James Brown is a former Australian Army officer, who commanded a cavalry troop in southern Iraq, served at the Australian taskforce headquarters in Baghdad and was attached to Special Forces in Afghanistan. He is the research director and an adjunct associate professor at the US Studies Centre, University of Sydney. He is the author of the acclaimed book *Anzac's Long Shadow*.

Jim Chalmers is a federal Labor MP. He has been director of the Chifley Research Centre, chief of staff to the deputy prime minister and treasurer, senior adviser to state and federal Labor leaders, and Labor's national research manager. His book *Glory Daze* was published in 2013.

Andrew Charlton is the author of *Ozonomics* and *Fair Trade for All* (with Joseph Stiglitz) and two Quarterly Essays, *Man-Made World* (which won the 2012 John Button Prize) and *Dragon's Tail*. From 2008 to 2010 he was senior economic adviser to Prime Minister Kevin Rudd. He is a director of the strategic advisory business AlphaBeta.

Saul Eslake is a vice-chancellor's fellow at the University of Tasmania and an independent consulting economist. He has previously been chief economist at ANZ, chief economist at Bank of America Merrill Lynch Australia, and director of the Productivity Growth Program at the Grattan Institute.

Verity Firth is the Executive Director, Social Justice at the University of Technology, Sydney. Before this she was chief executive of the Public Education Foundation and NSW Minister for Education and Training.

Elizabeth Humphrys is a political economist at the University of Technology, Sydney. In 2016 she completed her PhD thesis on *The Corporatist Origins of Neoliberalism: Australia's Accord, the Labour Movement and the Neoliberal Project*.

Bob Katter is a federal MP and the leader of Katter's Australian Party. He is the author of *An Incredible Race of People*.

George Megalogenis's books include *The Longest Decade*, *The Australian Moment* and *Australia's Second Chance*. His documentary *Making Australia Great: Inside Our Longest Boom* was screened on ABC TV in 2015. His previous Quarterly Essay was *Trivial Pursuit: Leadership and the End of the Reform Era*.

Clare O'Neil is a federal Labor MP. She studied economics at Harvard as a Fulbright Scholar and was Australia's youngest female mayor. She is the co-author, with Tim Watts, of *Two Futures*.

Henry Sherrell has been a policy analyst at the Migration Council and worked for the Department of Immigration and Citizenship. He is now an adviser to a federal MP.

Paul Strangio is an associate professor of politics at Monash University. His most recent book is *Settling the Office: The Australian Prime Ministership from Federation to Reconstruction* (co-authored with Paul 't Hart and James Walter).

Tad Tietze is a Sydney psychiatrist who co-runs the political blog *Left Flank*.

Jonathan West founded and directed Harvard's Life Sciences Project and the Australian Innovation Research Centre. He is the co-author, with Tom Bentley, of the Griffith REVIEW ebook *Time for a New Consensus*.

QUARTERLY ESSAY DIGITAL SUBSCRIPTIONS NOW AVAILABLE

SUBSCRIBE to Quarterly Essay & SAVE up to 25% on the cover price.

Enjoy free home delivery of the print edition and full digital access on the Quarterly Essay website, iPad, iPhone and Android apps.

FORTHCOMING ISSUES:

Don Watson on the American Election
September 2016

Stan Grant on Indigenous Futures
December 2016

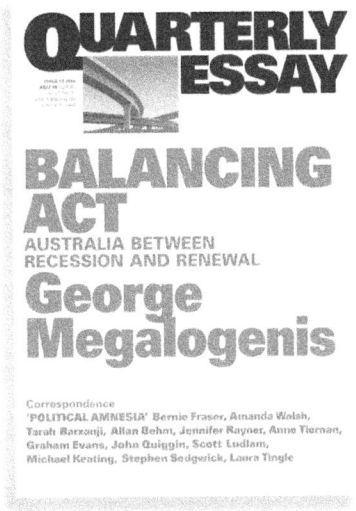

Subscriptions: Receive a discount and never miss an issue. Mailed direct to your door.
- ☐ **1 year print and digital subscription** (4 issues): $79.95 within Australia. Outside Australia $119.95
- ☐ **1 year print and digital gift subscription** (4 issues): $79.95 within Australia. Outside Australia $119.95
- ☐ **2 year print and digital subscription** (8 issues): $129.95 within Australia
- ☐ **2 year print and digital gift subscription** (8 issues): $129.95 within Australia
- ☐ **1 year digital only subscription** (4 issues): $39.95
- ☐ **1 year digital only gift subscription** (4 issues): $39.95

All prices include GST, postage and handling.

Please turn over for subscription order form, or subscribe online at **www.quarterlyessay.com**
Alternatively, call 1800 077 514 or 03 9486 0244, fax 03 9011 6106 or email subscribe@blackincbooks.com

Back Issues: (Prices include GST, postage and handling.)

- ☐ **QE 1** ($15.99) Robert Manne *In Denial*
- ☐ **QE 2** ($15.99) John Birmingham *Appeasing Jakarta*
- ☐ **QE 3** ($15.99) Guy Rundle *The Opportunist*
- ☐ **QE 4** ($15.99) Don Watson *Rabbit Syndrome*
- ☐ **QE 6** ($15.99) John Button *Beyond Belief*
- ☐ **QE 7** ($15.99) John Martinkus *Paradise Betrayed*
- ☐ **QE 8** ($15.99) Amanda Lohrey *Groundswell*
- ☐ **QE 9** ($15.99) Tim Flannery *Beautiful Lies*
- ☐ **QE 10** ($15.99) Gideon Haigh *Bad Company*
- ☐ **QE 11** ($15.99) Germaine Greer *Whitefella Jump Up*
- ☐ **QE 12** ($15.99) David Malouf *Made in England*
- ☐ **QE 13** ($15.99) Robert Manne with David Corlett *Sending Them Home*
- ☐ **QE 14** ($15.99) Paul McGeough *Mission Impossible*
- ☐ **QE 15** ($15.99) Margaret Simons *Latham's World*
- ☐ **QE 16** ($15.99) Raimond Gaita *Breach of Trust*
- ☐ **QE 17** ($15.99) John Hirst *'Kangaroo Court'*
- ☐ **QE 18** ($15.99) Gail Bell *The Worried Well*
- ☐ **QE 19** ($15.99) Judith Brett *Relaxed & Comfortable*
- ☐ **QE 20** ($15.99) John Birmingham *A Time for War*
- ☐ **QE 21** ($15.99) Clive Hamilton *What's Left?*
- ☐ **QE 22** ($15.99) Amanda Lohrey *Voting for Jesus*
- ☐ **QE 23** ($15.99) Inga Clendinnen *The History Question*
- ☐ **QE 24** ($15.99) Robyn Davidson *No Fixed Address*
- ☐ **QE 25** ($15.99) Peter Hartcher *Bipolar Nation*
- ☐ **QE 26** ($15.99) David Marr *His Master's Voice*
- ☐ **QE 27** ($15.99) Ian Lowe *Reaction Time*
- ☐ **QE 28** ($15.99) Judith Brett *Exit Right*
- ☐ **QE 29** ($15.99) Anne Manne *Love & Money*
- ☐ **QE 30** ($15.99) Paul Toohey *Last Drinks*
- ☐ **QE 31** ($15.99) Tim Flannery *Now or Never*
- ☐ **QE 32** ($15.99) Kate Jennings *American Revolution*
- ☐ **QE 33** ($15.99) Guy Pearse *Quarry Vision*
- ☐ **QE 34** ($15.99) Annabel Crabb *Stop at Nothing*
- ☐ **QE 35** ($15.99) Noel Pearson *Radical Hope*
- ☐ **QE 36** ($15.99) Mungo MacCallum *Australian Story*
- ☐ **QE 37** ($15.99) Waleed Aly *What's Right?*
- ☐ **QE 38** ($15.99) David Marr *Power Trip*
- ☐ **QE 39** ($15.99) Hugh White *Power Shift*
- ☐ **QE 40** ($15.99) George Megalogenis *Trivial Pursuit*
- ☐ **QE 41** ($15.99) David Malouf *The Happy Life*
- ☐ **QE 42** ($15.99) Judith Brett *Fair Share*
- ☐ **QE 43** ($15.99) Robert Manne *Bad News*
- ☐ **QE 44** ($15.99) Andrew Charlton *Man-Made World*
- ☐ **QE 45** ($15.99) Anna Krien *Us and Them*
- ☐ **QE 46** ($15.99) Laura Tingle *Great Expectations*
- ☐ **QE 47** ($15.99) David Marr *Political Animal*
- ☐ **QE 48** ($15.99) Tim Flannery *After the Future*
- ☐ **QE 49** ($15.99) Mark Latham *Not Dead Yet*
- ☐ **QE 50** ($15.99) Anna Goldsworthy *Unfinished Business*
- ☐ **QE 51** ($15.99) David Marr *The Prince*
- ☐ **QE 52** ($15.99) Linda Jaivin *Found in Translation*
- ☐ **QE 53** ($15.99) Paul Toohey *That Sinking Feeling*
- ☐ **QE 54** ($15.99) Andrew Charlton *Dragon's Tail*
- ☐ **QE 55** ($15.99) Noel Pearson *A Rightful Place*
- ☐ **QE 56** ($15.99) Guy Rundle *Clivosaurus*
- ☐ **QE 57** ($15.99) Karen Hitchcock *Dear Life*
- ☐ **QE 58** ($19.99) David Kilcullen *Blood Year*
- ☐ **QE 59** ($19.99) David Marr *Faction Man*
- ☐ **QE 60** ($22.99) Laura Tingle *Political Animal*
- ☐ **QE 61** ($22.99) George Megalogenis *Balancing Act*

☐ I enclose a cheque/money order made out to Schwartz Publishing Pty Ltd.
☐ Please debit my credit card (Mastercard, Visa or Amex accepted).

Card No. ☐☐☐☐ ☐☐☐☐ ☐☐☐☐ ☐☐☐☐

Expiry date ____/____ **CCV** _____ **Amount $** _____

Cardholder's name _____ **Signature** _____

Name _____

Address _____

Email _____ **Phone** _____

Post or fax this form to: Quarterly Essay, Reply Paid 90094, Carlton VIC 3053 / Freecall: 1800 077 514
Tel: (03) 9486 0288 / Fax: (03) 9011 6106 / Email: subscribe@blackincbooks.com
Subscribe online at **www.quarterlyessay.com**

www.ingramcontent.com/pod-product-compliance
Lightning Source LLC
Chambersburg PA
CBHW080639170426
43200CB00015B/2901